D0856364

Corporate Fraud

The Human Factor

Corporate Fraud

The Human Factor

Maryam Hussain

B L O O M S B U R Y

LONDON · NEW DELHI · NEW YORK · SYDNEY

First published in United Kingdom in 2014 by

Bloomsbury Publishing Plc
50 Bedford Square
London
WC1B 3DP
www.bloomsbury.com

Copyright © Maryam Hussain, 2014
All rights reserved; no part of this publication may be reproduced, stored in a
retrieval system, or transmitted by any means, electronic, mechanical, photocopying
or otherwise, without the prior written permission of the Publisher.

No responsibility for loss caused to any individual or organisation acting
or refraining from action as a result of the material in this publication
can be accepted by Bloomsbury Publishing or the authors.

A CIP record for this book is available from the British Library.

ISBN: 9781472905086

This book is produced using paper that is made from wood grown in managed,
sustainable forests. It is natural, renewable and recyclable. The logging and manufacturing
processes conform to the environmental regulations of the country of origin.

Design by Fiona Pike, Pike Design, Winchester
Typeset by Hewer Text UK Ltd, Edinburgh
Printed and bound in Great Britain by CPI Group (UK) Ltd, Croydon CR0 4YY

Contents

Foreword

Businesses today are operating in an extremely challenging environment. Growth potential is minimal or sluggish in many established markets and companies are searching for growth in new, and higher risk, markets.

The regulatory enforcement environment is changing too. Aggressive prosecution of bribery and corruption is increasing the risk of operating in many new markets. Yet these are often the same markets which are critical to business growth and establishing a sustainable supply chain.

Bribery and corruption is not the only heightened risk as a result of tough economic conditions. Pressure to deliver financial results elevates a broad range of fraud risks – from financial statement fraud to "rogue trading" and embezzlement. For some businesses, this heightened risk is combined with vulnerabilities in the control environment as a result of substantial cost cutting on control and oversight functions.

Looking to the future, we see continued cross-border enforcement in relation to bribery and corruption. Improved cooperation amongst national regulators and law enforcement agencies will increase the likelihood of costly parallel investigations with multiple regulators, resulting in significant fines. And derivative actions by regulators in emerging markets – as we are already seeing in Africa and Asia – may become commonplace.

In addition, in the age of social media, fraud and corruption in the furthest corner of an organisation, can quickly become headline news around the world. Whistleblowing is more prevalent and rewards and protections for whistleblowers are becoming enshrined in legislation.

Corporate and personal reputations for integrity and trust built over many generations can be tainted in an instant.

It is in this context that the EY Fraud Investigation & Dispute Services practice (FIDS), with more than 2,400 professionals in over 60 countries, supports our clients to investigate and fight fraud and corruption.

Every instance of fraud and corruption leaves a trail which is visible but often unseen until it is too late. By seeing organisations from the fraudsters' perspective and learning lessons of the past, vulnerabilities can be identified and guide the design of detection mechanisms and response to incidents of fraud and corruption. In this book we draw on our team's global experience, in addition to those of senior executives, law enforcement and regulatory authorities, to bring the "fraud trail" into sharp focus - and to provide a practical guide for government and business leaders on managing fraud risk.

David Stulb
January 2014

David Stulb is the Global Leader for EY's Fraud Investigation & Dispute Services practice. He has extensive experience leading complex investigations in Europe, Middle East, Asia, Africa and the Americas. Before joining EY, David served as the Global Partner-in-Charge of the Business Fraud and Investigation Services for Arthur Andersen LLP, where he had a prominent role in the investigation of Enron.

Preface

What is corporate fraud?

The 1990s: a decade marked by global recession following the US savings and loans crisis. This was the decade when forensic accountancy really came into its own. Now, nearly 20 years on, we have drawn on the experience of over 70 investigators from around the world, to give a practical perspective on corporate fraud – the fraudsters, their motivations and how they penetrate sophisticated systems without detection. This journey begins by looking back on some of the most notable corporate frauds and the lessons that organisations fail to learn and the fraudsters exploit.

Early beginnings – the South Sea Company

One of the earliest and most notable corporate frauds concerned a British company that was founded in the early 18th century. The story of the company and the asset price bubble to which it gave its name has all the elements: corruption, insider dealing and fraudulent accounting.

As a company with limited real trading activity, the South Sea Company was nevertheless the subject of an incredible frenzy of speculation that was supported by spreading rumours of success, buying the influence of politicians, exploiting insider information on impending government decisions and complex schemes, which included financing the dealing in its own shares. Driven by this activity, the price of its shares rocketed almost ten-fold during 1720. Similar share price gains were seen for companies established during the same period; companies which ranged from legitimate enterprises to those created specifically to exploit the stock market frenzy and gullibility and greed of private investors.

The bubble deflated as rapidly as it had expanded, as a combination of adverse market conditions and the unwinding of supporting schemes resulted in a self-perpetuating spiral of asset depreciation and investor bankruptcy. There followed criminal and civil actions against directors, financiers and politicians. From the South Sea Bubble in the early 18th century to Madoff in the early 21st – there is a simple lesson: if performance appears to defy the markers or simple logic, then investors should ask more challenging questions as the story may not be all it seems.

The Match King

To many fraud investigators, the story of the 'Match King' of the early 20th century provides rich insights into the dynamics of the fraudster and his victims. The eponymous fraudster, Ivar Kreuger, built and ran a vast empire of companies spanning finance and construction. His nickname of 'Match King' was earned through his activities in the safety match industry, which he monopolised across the world during the 1920s – monopolies achieved through loan deals with nation states that had become impoverished through the post-war recession. The audacious financial engineering that he deployed was the mark of a man often described as a genius by the writers of the time.

But his success was not all that it appeared. Apparently under huge financial pressure, Kreuger committed suicide in 1932, and it was only then that the array of methods that he used to sustain his empire was uncovered. Kreuger had used a series of innovative financial constructs, many of which were to later reappear in both legitimate and fraudulent enterprises. One example, which was a central feature of the Enron case, was the use of 'off-balance sheet' companies to disguise the group's huge debts. The other was less subtle and involved drawing down loans to make interest and dividend payments – a scheme that echoed in the Madoff scandal more than 70 years later. The uncovering of these schemes, and the financial black holes that they created resulted in the

'Kreuger crash' as thousands of investors found their shareholdings to be worthless.

Perhaps the most significant effect of the Kreuger scandal was its influence over the creation of the US Securities and Exchange Commission by the 1934 Securities Exchange Act and the earlier Securities Act of 1933. These acts, which were also a response to the unreliability of financial information that was a feature of the time, started to define a regime of more open, transparent and reliable financial reporting to help investors make better informed decisions.

The evolution of the accounting standards underpinning better financial reporting has continued to present day – although throughout a period punctuated by further accounting scandals. In 2002, after the collapse of WorldCom following fraudulent accounting which disguised a $3.8bn 'hole' in the company's performance, a former WorldCom accountant summed up the situation: "There is a perception that accounting is black and white. In fact it is all shades of grey." Where the 'numbers' are at odds with the market conditions and commercial reality, too often victims of fraud believe the numbers.

Parmalat

Another recent accounting scandal concerns an Italian company Parmalat SpA, which collapsed in 2003. Initially, the accounting 'black hole' was estimated at €8bn, but after years of investigation the total debt was found to be more that €14bn. The story was one that will be familiar to those that follow the rise and eventual fall of such corporate giants.

Starting small in the 1960s, Parmalat grew to prominence as a producer of a range of dairy products and through its specialisation in the production of UHT milk. Made famous by its sponsorship of various Formula 1 teams and drivers, Parmalat was listed on the Milan stock exchange in 1990 and continued to grow through a series of acquisitions to become a huge global corporation.

But the story came to an abrupt end in 2003 as a combination of the costs of its debt-fuelled expansion and the worsening performance of many of its divisions pushed elements of its management to a range of inappropriate financial engineering. These included the use of complex derivatives to create the illusion of assets. Ultimately, as is often the case, it was the inability to raise any more cash which triggered the collapse. The founder and CEO, Calisto Tanzi, was charged with fraud and money-laundering and sentenced to 10 years imprisonment.

Charles Ponzi

As Ivar Kreuger was building his empire in the early 1920s, he may have observed the uncovering of another extraordinary fraudster after whom an entire class of fraud was named – Charles Ponzi.

Ponzi promised extraordinary gains to those willing to invest in his scheme which he claimed was built on lucrative trading in postal reply coupons. This get-rich-quick scheme attracted investors who received the expected high returns, as Ponzi simply paid them from receipts from later investors. The more word spread, the more investors his scheme attracted – Ponzi created a company and employed agents to find more and more investors.

The scheme grew rapidly, making Ponzi a very rich man. But its failure was inevitable, as the requirement to repay early investors started to exceed his ability to attract new cash as suspicions grew about the scheme. When the crash came, investors found that their holdings were worth a small fraction of what they expected and several financial institutions collapsed in the fall out.

The Ponzi, or 'pyramid' scheme, as it is also known, has been repeated many times on small and massive scales. During the 1990s, Albania's entire economy was virtually destroyed by schemes in which almost the whole population participated, as rival banks outbid each other with higher and higher interest rates that were ultimately unsustainable. Later, in 2008, one of this century's most renowned fraudsters, Bernard Madoff, was found to have presided over an enormous Ponzi scheme that, whilst appearing to be more sophisticated than any of those that preceded it, nevertheless followed the well-worn path of paying investors with later investors' cash.

The cases of Charles Ponzi and Bernard Madoff represent a variation on the theme of 'if it's too good to be true . . .' The lesson is not to be taken in by early returns – it may be a trap to draw in the initially sceptical investor.

Barings Bank

In 1995, an altogether different type of corporate fraud brought down one of Britain's oldest banks. Nick Leeson was a financial trader who was employed by Barings Bank to run its Singapore trading operations. Shortly after arriving in Singapore, Leeson started to make unauthorised trades that initially made large profits for his employer. However, when later trading was less successful, Leeson used one of the bank's 'error accounts' to hide his losses – a technique that he was able to exploit as he had responsibility for both making and settling his trades, breaching the principle of segregation of front- and back-office duties, which is used to prevent such abuses.

Leeson's losses grew as he placed increasingly risky and ever-larger trades – such losses running to tens and then hundreds of millions of pounds. Eventually, as a result of a market crash precipitated by a huge earthquake in Japan, Leeson's losses became too massive to hide. In early 1995, Barings Bank discovered that Leeson had hidden losses of over £800m, substantially exceeding the bank's available capital and rendering it insolvent.

Many lessons were learned from this affair, as systems were improved and a greater level of scrutiny was placed on traders and their activities. But Leeson's case illustrates the dangers of placing too much trust and knowledge in one person's hands. As other banks have found to their cost, there have been many 'Leesons' over the years – traders able to use their intimate knowledge of the systems and controls placed around them to obscure unauthorised trades, mask losses and misrepresent themselves as massively successful 'star' traders.

One of the most persistent of the myths and misunderstandings about fraud and fraudsters in companies is that 'our people would not commit fraud' and 'we'd know quickly if it happened, we watch the vulnerable areas'. But fraud is about people and their motivations. From Scott Sullivan, the former CFO of WorldCom who pleaded guilty to conspiracy, securities fraud and making false financial filings, who said, "It was a misguided effort to save the company" to Madoff's reflections that, "I was upset with the whole idea of not being in the [Wall Street insiders club]" and that "Everyone was greedy. I just went along."[1]

The lessons from cases dating back to the 18th century, is that fraudsters are endlessly ingenious, in securing trust so that they can bypass sophisticated systems, controls and people's better judgements. The key is to be alert to the warning signs, which are all too visible with the benefit of hindsight.

---

1. http://www.ibtimes.com/select-quotes-bernard-madoff-magazine-interview-271615

Chapter 1

Introduction

"I just didn't expect it to be *them*," is the common reaction when fraudsters are uncovered. We see what we expect to see. Psychologists call it 'confirmation bias' – actively seeking out evidence that confirms our expectations and ignoring that which does not. Every fraud leaves a trail, but we do not expect to be victims and so do not see the tell-tale signs until the fraud is so big that it cannot be ignored. We also know that once something is raised in our consciousness – a brand or famous face, for example – we become more aware of it and see it everywhere. The same applies to fraud schemes. Experienced fraud investigators are often able to recognise early signs which others may miss.

This is not an academic text book on fraud. We have drawn on decades of the practical experience of fraud investigators from around the world and present a distilled perspective on fraud risk management, detection and investigation. Our objective is to enable you to look at your organisation through a new lens, one that magnifies the signs that you may have otherwise missed, leaving you better equipped to react to the discovery of fraud and to better guard against fraudsters in the future.

So who's on the 'other side'? Who are the fraudsters? What values define them? How do you spot a fraud and its trail before it's too late? And, once found, how do you take the first steps in the investigation which may lead to tracking down the stolen assets? These are questions that we will answer in this book.

Some fraudsters have achieved almost mythical status. Films have been made about them, bestsellers have been written and the public has been gripped by the unfolding of their dramatic stories. Does examining these 'legends' and their crimes instruct us on the kind of people we should be on the look out for? Or are these extraordinary characters that, but for a personality flaw or a particular set of circumstances, could have been honest and successful leaders of reputable organisations? And how can we discriminate between the 'good' and the 'bad'?

What about the more 'ordinary' fraudsters? How do you distinguish the potential rogue employee from those that behave with legality and integrity? As we will explain, this represents a significant challenge; as, given the incentive and opportunity and an ability to rationalise their actions, almost anyone is capable of committing fraud.

If there is no way of identifying a fraudster based on a set of objective characteristics or a particular socio-economic profile, what about the influence of the organisation itself? How should we take into account the culture and values upon which it is founded? It is often the case that a narrowly defined objective – an ever-growing sales target to achieve a bonus, a consistent progression of earnings per share to maintain an upward trending share price – takes precedence over everything else and can lead to employees stepping over the line to achieve the goals that they have been set (or set themselves). Such potentially harmful, one-dimensional targets can be identified relatively easily. But what about more apparently 'benevolent' values such as social responsibility or employee protection? Can these be taken to an extreme where unexpectedly adverse consequences result in the playing of the corporate equivalent of the 'trump card' to bypass the myriad of systems and controls?

With no guaranteed way of preventing future 'rogue employees' from entering the organisation, companies will need to be sure that their fraud prevention and detection systems are up to the challenge. The first line of defence for the organisation is people, including employees, customers and suppliers, who blow the whistle. But, closely followed by automated tools to spot the trails of fraud at an early stage through forensic data analytics.

It is the combination of the use of technology and an environment that encourages whistleblowers to step forward which creates the strongest protection against fraudsters. This is promoted through clear communication of the right values and unambiguous actions.

Other detection strategies include establishing and promoting a capable, respected and independent internal audit function which can challenge established practices in every corner of the organisation – including at senior levels and in remote locations. This may be enhanced by using technology to spot the warning signs of known fraud schemes and patterns pointing to newly emerging threats. However, both internal audit and the use of technology can provide false comfort if deployed with either a weak mandate or inadequate technical skills.

Once a fraud investigation is under way, if poorly executed the investigation can cause more damage, for example, tipping off the fraudster at a stage when he can destroy documents and abscond with stolen assets. The immediate response to a fraud investigation must be pitch-perfect, with an investigation team equipped with the resources, knowledge and tools to avoid the pitfalls and give the organisation the best prospect of a successful outcome. Independent expertise and oversight – including external legal counsel – may be required and, if evidence of fraud is found, decisions need to be made on when and how to involve the police or regulators whilst taking action to minimise the loss and damage to the organisation.

As soon as a theft of assets is identified, the race is on to try to get them back. The imperative of a fraudster is to put as much distance, and as many barriers, as possible between the stolen assets and the organisation. Today, cash may be moved through layers of bank accounts and across borders in a matter of hours; shell companies or off-shore trusts may be used to create a tangled web designed to obscure the source, destination and ownership of funds; intellectual property enters the cloud, protected by passwords, firewalls and the anonymity that cyberspace provides.

In response, organisations can deploy both legal instruments and technology to peel away the layers of deception. Banking data may be mined to reveal the flows of funds and the powers of the insolvency practitioner may be used to chip away at the fraudsters' defences. In the case of data theft, firewall logs and other electronic trails can be examined to provide clues to the destination of stolen information.

However, time is of the essence and organisations need to move quickly and decisively to recover stolen funds. In the aftermath of a major fraud, the organisation will also need to focus on business as usual.

Employees will feel uncertainty and will seek reassurance. Such reassurance is delivered by clear messages about the future from a strong leadership team, including the acknowledgement that lessons will be learned and the necessary changes will be made. These can be seen in incremental improvements in controls or even wholesale replacement of fundamentally flawed systems or processes, or the requirement for changes in the culture of the organisation. Loopholes in detection mechanisms may have become apparent as a result of the fraud. The experience of fraud may also cause the organisation to revaluate how it hires, trains and motivates its employees.

Looking forward, new threats are emerging which put even more pressure on organisations' defences. The same technology that is transforming the method and speed with which business is conducted can be turned against organisations. Cybercriminals are becoming ever more sophisticated, and organisations need new strategies to stay one step ahead of them and fight back swiftly when attacked.

The ongoing Great Recession is also weighing heavily on the defences of organisations, particularly in the mature economies. Employees who feel that their prosperity is being eroded by limited pay rises and diminishing or non-existent bonuses may believe they are justified to take what they consider to be rightfully theirs. The threat of redundancy or insolvency can also drive individuals at all levels to manipulate financial results or hide bad news to forestall impending disaster.

With little prospect of growth in mature economies, organisations are looking to emerging markets. There, they then discover that the size and shape of the fraud threat is very different. We will share insights from experienced fraud risk investigators in Africa, India, China and the Middle East to illustrate some of the ways in which these differences manifest themselves.

And what of the future? As far back as 31 BC, Caesar Augustus imposed heavy penalties on fraudsters found using gold-plated bronze to forge 'pure' gold coins. Will tomorrow's fraud threats really look very different to those that organisations face today? We are not futurologists, but we will provide you with our perspective on where we anticipate changes and, indeed, where change is perhaps less likely. We will also consider the changes that may be required to strategies of fraud prevention, detection and investigation that such a future state demands.

But one thing is for sure: in the words of Diana Henriques, the first reporter to interview Bernard Madoff in jail, "No fraud deterrence program, however elaborate, will work if it can be switched off for the people we trust most." We expect and trust people to do the right thing. In this book we will share our experience of investigating those who betrayed the trust placed in them – and the 'early warning signs' that were there all along but were missed until it was too late.

Chapter 2

Approaches to fraud risk

Introduction

Business is all about the balance between risk and reward. With higher risk comes greater reward – higher profits, increased market share, faster share price growth – provided the risks are well managed. This means that organisations are constantly assessing how much of a diverse set of risks they can profitably accept; they extend credit to their customers, buy stock with the expectation of selling it for a profit and draw down loans for investment with the confidence that they will generate sufficient revenues to both pay their debts and realise a healthy return.

Fraud should be just one of the many risks that organisations manage in their day-to-day operations, but it is often seen as a remote risk – 'it doesn't happen here'. But to make a realistic assessment of fraud risks, an organisation has to answer the difficult question of 'how could it happen here?' One reason for the difficulty in answering this is, as we will discuss in the next chapter, that perpetrators of fraud are often individuals who are amongst the most trusted people in the organisation, and challenging such individuals, who may have been part of the team for many years, can place management in a very uncomfortable position.

Senior management of any commercial organisation have a clear view on how they will make the next million Euros of profit. What is often less clear to them is what their organisation needs to do to guard against becoming the victim of the next million Euro fraud. Companies are focussed on hiring the best sales people or product developers – the identification and recruitment of specialists in compliance or fraud risk management is likely to be much further down the list of priorities. The challenge, then, for an organisation is to think more broadly about their strategy: fraud risk should be considered at the same time as evaluating commercial prospects such as new market entry, product development and customer targeting.

In this chapter we explore the nature of fraud risk, why internal controls are only part of the answer to managing this risk and the role of the different functions in an organisation: from the board to the employees.

The challenge with fraud

Fraud is a complex and dynamic risk that presents a challenge to any organisation in any industry. The only limit to the types and mechanisms for fraud is the ingenuity of people – and this is why there is an infinite variety of fraud risks, which vary in response to changes in the organisation or in its markets. It is also very difficult to measure progress in dealing with fraud risk – is success 'constant vigilance and nothing happens' or the achievement of a target rate of fraud detection? And who is ultimately responsible for ensuring that the risks of fraud are addressed – the board? the management team? These are some of the factors that contribute to the complexity of dealing with fraud risk.

Defining fraud

There are many definitions of fraud and corruption. Five of the largest international development banks[1] developed the following definitions for the purposes of a mutual enforcement agreement.

- A *corrupt* practice is the offering, giving, receiving or soliciting, directly or indirectly, of anything of value to influence improperly the actions of another party.

- A *fraudulent* practice is any act or omission, including a misrepresentation, that knowingly or recklessly misleads, or attempts to mislead, a party to obtain a financial or other benefit or to avoid an obligation.

This definition is helpful as a starting point for assessing an organisation's exposure to fraud risk.

Defining fraud risk

At one end of the spectrum, there are frauds that are small in their monetary impact, but relatively high in frequency – falsification of invoices, fabrication of expense claims or payment of small kickbacks to secure contracts. These 'ordinary' frauds, as we describe them, may be committed by individuals at any level in the organisation. Their prevalence could, over time, erode profits and undermine the culture of the organisation, but are unlikely to be a threat to the ongoing existence of the organisation.

At the other end of the scale, there are frauds that occur rarely but have a very significant detrimental impact on the organisation, perhaps threatening its independence or even its very survival. These are the 'extraordinary' frauds that are most often committed by senior management and which tend to be complex and organised in nature. In addition to the large sums that are at stake, such frauds can fatally undermine third parties' confidence in the integrity of the organisation.

There are, of course, frauds which are somewhere in the middle of the spectrum – small enough that the company survives, but nevertheless significantly newsworthy that they become public knowledge and adversely impact the organisation's image and operations. All of these different classes of fraud are related – an organisation that either ignores or fails properly to address the ordinary frauds is more likely eventually to find itself the victim of an extraordinary event. A level of vigilance on the smaller frauds can play a vital role in dealing with the overall risk of fraud through fostering a pervasive anti-fraud culture within the organisation. The legal consequences of some frauds, such as bribery, can be very serious even if the amounts involved are small, a feature which is becoming increasingly significant as the world's regulators and law enforcement agencies focus their attention on corruption and corporate misconduct. We will return to these subjects later in this chapter.

An ever-changing landscape

Once an organisation has understood its vulnerabilities to different types of fraud and the nature of the risks to which it is exposed – we will look at some of the ways an organisation can identify these – one thing which is certain is that these risks will continue to change over time. Fraud is an incredibly dynamic risk that will not remain static for long – changes can come from a number of directions. A merger or acquisition, for example, will introduce new operating practices and business cultures to the organisation; entering a new market can similarly have disruptive consequences. As fraud risks change, the organisation will need to adapt in order to protect itself.

The changes highlighted above are the result of choices that are made by the organisation, but there are other factors that will always be outside of its control. As we will discuss later in the book, the relentless march of technology is introducing an entirely new range of risks, and macro-economic forces are dramatically shifting the goal posts. It is in this context that governments, regulators and society look to global organisations to spot the rogue employee or operation long before it has the power to bring down the organisation with the corresponding economic impact.

Measurement of success

'Return on investment' is a fundamental part of how organisations make decisions on where to direct attention and allocate their limited resources. The challenge of defining the return on investment on anti-fraud initiatives stems from traditional methods of seeking to measure an outcome – such as increased fraud detection rates – as opposed to also focusing on the consequences of not protecting the organisation. For example, in an organisation with a profit margin of 10%, a loss of €100,000 will wipe out profits from an increase in sales of €1m. If we consider how much effort would have to be expended to drive such an increase in sales, anti-fraud efforts will start to make sense, even to the most sceptical sales director.

Other, often neglected, consequences of an incident of fraud or bribery include exclusion from tender lists (of public sector organisations, for example) and the withdrawal of licences or rights to trade in entire markets or to sell certain products. Cross-debarment agreements between the World Bank and four other development banks, are intended to incentivise ethical behaviour by preventing those organisations found to be involved in dishonest behaviour from accessing significant opportunities and markets. The impact of such agreements is yet to be fully realised. Commentary published in 2012 by one of the banks, the Asian Development Bank, highlighted the fact that within the first two years of their existence, the number of firms and individuals that had been debarred included 79 firms and 51 individuals[2]. The names of such debarred or sanctioned entities are published through the 'Cross Debarment' website[3].

But perhaps the costliest consequence is the loss of reputation or customer confidence, which can persist for a long time following a major incident of fraud or corruption – more so now, with the prevalence of social media and global communications, than ever before. As Cynthia Schoeman, a senior adviser in the field of workplace ethics puts it, "All these costs cumulatively contribute to a legacy cost, and this is a cost which can linger and cast a shadow over an individual or an organisation long after the event. Serious ethical failure such as corruption tends to outshine other achievements, and the individual or organisation comes to be known for their ethical failure rather than their success."

In this context, the key question in dedicating resources to protect an organisation from fraud and corruption is, 'What is the price of our reputation?'

Assessing fraud risk

There are many complex fraud risk assessment models with a myriad of fraud types and methodologies to measure potential impact. Anti-fraud practitioners view many of these models as detracting from the simple questions that should help to focus anti-fraud activities. Management need to consider what is going to cause it the most significant problems – what could damage the organisation's brand or endanger its licence to operate. Many companies focus on the smaller details. There are companies doing background due diligence on every single supplier they work with globally, which is excessive. The question they need to consider is whether the rogue small supplier represents the greater risk. The results of such due diligence are provided to operational managers who may not know now to interpret the information.

In order to focus effort and attention, organisations often start by considering the fraud risks that are relevant to their industry. These will vary considerably from sector to sector. The threats faced by an insurance company will reflect the risk of fraudulent claims or the improper under-pricing of insurance premiums; a pharmaceutical company will be more concerned with protecting its intellectual property, preventing counterfeit product from entering the market and unethical sales practices. An organisation should consider the areas where it is most exposed. Perhaps this is the loss of cash through fraudulent invoices or having ghost employees on the payroll. It must also consider the specific regulations under which it operates.

Monetary loss as a result of fraud is typically the greatest concern for a company, but to focus only on this may be overlooking other, potentially more serious problems, such as the theft of intellectual property that is inherent to its ongoing existence. This risk is not confined to high-tech products. For example, a food manufacturer decided to separate preparation of its branded meals to different sites so that no site had access to entire recipies.

To make sensible decisions on what resources need to be devoted to fraud mitigation strategies, fraud risk assessment must consider both the potential impact and the likelihood of any given threat. And the 'costs' may be much more than simply the amount of money taken or the recorded value of the intellectual property that is stolen.

Controlling fraud risk

The problem with controls

Controls are only effective if they are frequently aligned to the risks and updated to account for changing circumstances. When it comes to fraud, failure of internal controls is only part of the story. There is no universal foolproof control against fraud. Organisations need to deploy a different way of thinking about fraud and about how to protect themselves. Building more and more rules and layers of mechanistic procedures is rarely effective. An organisation can put every single possible control in place, but if the management structures and business environment are not conducive, the formal controls will have little impact. In some of the biggest fraud cases, the root cause of the fraud was that the employees were getting a clear message about what was *really* valued – for example, sales, profits at all costs – despite contrary public statements. Formal controls will have little impact in such a corporate culture.

Strict conformity with controls can give a false sense of security to risk and compliance managers, who regard it as a convenient 'comfort blanket' for a company that wants to be able to show that it has fraud risk covered. These controls amount to a series or aggregate of fixed and narrow procedures, leading, it is hoped, to an inevitable, even predictable, outcome. But, as we have seen, fraud risk is not a structured and easily defined concept: in fact, it is unstructured, highly imprecise and very dynamic. The greatest risk arises from the behaviour and intentions of managers and executives, wrestling with many unpredictable internal and external pressures.

The limited benefit of controls operating in the absence of an effective culture of fraud awareness and appropriate scepticism is illustrated by considering the case where the staff have complied with every letter of the procedures. The right people signed off on a transaction with the right delegation of authority with all the right paperwork in place. But in reality, the organisation should never have entered into the transaction. Organisations should focus on the underlying business activity, and ensure that the controls do not simply become an exercise in box-ticking. The "informal control" of properly trained staff operating in a corporate culture which promotes ethical behaviour, has vastly more impact in managing fraud risk than a myriad of "formal contracts".

Creating the right environment

The chances that internal controls will be effective at reducing the incidence of fraud are critically dependent upon the culture that pervades the organisation – that culture drives the decisions and behaviours of employees at all levels. In turn, that culture is dependent upon the governance of the organisation and the way in which individuals throughout the organisation fulfil their respective roles and responsibilities, and articulate and respect its values.

Culture

An organisation's culture provide a framework which guides the way management and employees think, feel and act in their day to day work-related activities. Culture is established by tangible measures such as a widely publicised mission statement or set of written values. This has to be underpinned by behavioural aspects such as the example set by senior management and how the company deals with third parties such as customers and suppliers. The culture of an organisation will have a significant bearing on its performance to the extent that it drives business activity.

The cultural message must also be consistent in a global company. The values implicit in an ethical culture should not be at odds with the practice. If, for example, the company states as a key value the need for transparency and integrity, it cannot encourage its employees to unfairly undermine competitors. Likewise, if the organisation preaches long-termisim, it cannot put pressure on employees to push risk-taking to the limit in pursuit of the next sales targets. Such mixed messages in fact send another clear message: disregard what we say, focus on what we reward.

One company manager explains the impact of confusing messages: "The setting of objectives and performance appraisals needs to be consistent with the company's ethics, values and incentives, and rewards need to be in line with what the business is trying to do. It is frequently the case, especially in banks and in pharmaceuticals, that incentives actually operate in the opposite direction to ethics and values; incentives will almost always trump the values, either because the incentives are too great or people will look at their incentives and think, 'Well, you clearly want me to deliver, you are saying all this stuff, but you've made it very clear what my targets are and you are incentivising me to make them.'"

This inconsistency between theory and practice has a very acute and damaging impact on an employee's behaviour. Where senior managers are pushed to make ever greater returns for their department or division, there is the risk that a point will be reached where they feel that they cannot meet those expectations through following legitimate methods. Under such circumstances they might decide to buy themselves some breathing room by falsely revaluing their inventory upwards, by delaying some payments to suppliers or through booking sales a little earlier. This may work once, but the next target might stretch them even further and the measures that they will need to take will become even more significant and the fraud will grow.

Who does what?

All those who work within an organisation have a role to play in maintaining the defences against the threat of fraud.

Board of directors

Members of the board have both legal and practical responsibilities in relation to the conduct of their organisation and its employees. Across all regions, existing or anticipated legislation has established what is expected of directors in the context of fraud and corruption, and defined the sanctions that may be imposed on them if they are shown to have failed in their duties.

In the UK, for example, the Bribery Act 2010 has defined corporate and director liability, although cases such as that faced by Mabey & Johnson Ltd, prosecuted under the pre-existing legislation, have shown how severe potential penalties can be.

Mabey & Johnson – a lesson on director responsibility

Mabey & Johnson Ltd was the first company successfully prosecuted in the UK for overseas corruption. The details of the corruption appear to have come to light as a result of allegations made by a former Mabey & Johnson manager in the course of his defence against litigation, brought by Mabey & Johnson.

Mabey & Johnson had entered into a contract to supply 13 bridges under the UN Oil-for-Food-programme, a scheme introduced to alleviate the hardship of the Iraqi people. Illegal kickback payments of over £420,000 secured the contract and represented 10% of the contract value. This kickback was required to be paid before products could cross the Iraqi border, so that Mabey & Johnson could fulfil the terms of the contract.

The kickback was represented as 'commission' payable to Mabey & Johnson's local representative, Upper Gulf Agencies (UGA), and added on to the contract value. Mabey & Johnson did not, as a result, bear the cost of making this kickback payment. Richard Gledhill, a sales manager for Mabey & Johnson, negotiated the contract with the Iraqi government and obtained approval to make the kickback payments from two of Mabey & Johnson's directors, Charles Forsyth and David Mabey.

It was an offence to make funds available to the Iraqi government without the authority of a licence granted by Her Majesty's Treasury, and no licence had been applied for by Mabey & Johnson. Mabey & Johnson itself pleaded guilty to violating UN sanctions. It was fined £6.6m and submitted its internal compliance programme to a Serious Fraud Office (SFO) approved independent monitor.

The SFO continued to investigate the roles of Gledhill, Mabey and Forsyth, and each was subsequently charged with breaching UN sanctions. Gledhill, the former sales manager, pleaded guilty and gave evidence for the prosecution. He received an eight-month prison sentence, suspended for two years. The Crown Court jury also convicted Forsyth and Mabey, and each received a prison sentence. Judge Rivlin said of David Mabey, "When a director of a major company plays even a small part [in corrupt activity], he can expect to receive a custodial sentence."

Richard Alderman, the then Director of the SFO, said of the guilty plea, "These are serious offences and it is significant that Mabey & Johnson has cooperated with us to get to this landmark point. This has enabled this case to be dealt with in just over a year, and is a model for other companies who want to self-report corruption and have it dealt with quickly and fairly by the SFO."

In addition to legal requirements, the board has the practical responsibility of nurturing an ethically sound environment. This is realised through developing what is often referred to as an appropriate 'tone at the top', a clear message of the organisation's values and a statement that inappropriate behaviour will not be tolerated. This is achieved through consistency in words and actions – setting and following the right ethical framework. The most visible example of this is often seen in the way that leadership openly (and loudly) promotes messages in relation to whistleblower hotlines or regulatory compliance. A personal message from the CEO expressing support and encouragement for such initiatives might, for example, be deployed on posters, intranet sites and video screens throughout the organisation.

Non-executive directors

Non-executive directors are, in many ways, well suited to critically assessing how the organisation deals with fraud risk, as they have the power and duty to hold directors to account. The board and its committees have the scope not only to monitor corporate risk and its impact on stakeholders, but also to set high-level expectations and standards. Such standards look outwards and reflect prevailing risks in the context of the organisation. The responsibility for managing this risk ultimately falls to the board.

Non-executive directors also have a key responsibility to maintain the anti-fraud risk culture and controls. The role of the non-executives is to ask the head of internal audit or IT risk, 'Can you tell me what fraud cases have happened this year and how have you dealt with them?' 'What other areas should I be concerned about?' 'Where do we need additional resources to manage fraud risks?' Non executives will be an important lobby for allocating investment to counter-fraud budgets which have come under severe pressure as a result of reductions in compliance and other budgets.

Directors and non-executives are required to be proactive. The role of a non-executive is very difficult, particularly in conglomerates with a multitude of businesses, in different industries which carry different risks. A key element of governance is for the board to challenge executive directors and managers about ethics, responsibilities and transparency. This serves as a control over some key fraud risks, in particular that of the dominating chief executive who holds all around him in fear. For example, they might be faced with considering the risks where the division is trading commodities in Europe, whilst another is constructing infrastructure in an emerging market where it needs to obtain licences from the government. The Satyam case, which is covered in more detail in chapter 8, demonstrates the consequences of such a disconnection between those at the top of the organisation and those lower down. There, the problems might have been discovered much earlier if managers had been asked about the performance of their divisions.

The non-executive director has a wide-ranging and ever-growing range of responsibilities. In addition to dealing with past problems, they need to ensure that the company is equipped to avoid problems in the future. The personal risks that face such individuals are becoming greater as legislation such as the UK Bribery Act and the US Foreign Corrupt Practices Act is replicated across the globe.

Audit committee

One of the ways in which non-executive directors fulfil their fraud risk management brief is through serving on the audit committee. Sometimes more accurately referred to as the 'audit and risk committee', the audit committee has a significant role to play in the context of addressing all risks facing the organisation, including those relating to fraud and corruption. Whilst not expected to carry out functions that belong to others, which would undermine the committee's essential independence, it is expected to obtain a clear understanding of what management is doing to prevent and detect fraud and corruption.

The UK's Financial Reporting Council's (FRC) guidance[4] includes a definition of what roles and responsibilities should be included within an audit committee's terms of reference. This is summarised as follows:

- Monitor financial statements and announcements.
- Review the internal controls.
- Monitor the effectiveness of internal audit.
- Carry out specific actions in relation to the appointment, remuneration and independence of external auditors.

There are other specific responsibilities including the review and assessment of the effectiveness of the organisation's whistleblowing arrangements, and also ensuring that incidents and allegations of fraud and corruption are appropriately dealt with. In carrying out such responsibilities, an independent audit committee can represent a clear deterrent to those throughout the organisation.

Given its responsibilities, independence is a fundamental attribute of the audit committee – any indication that such independence is in doubt would significantly undermine the audit committee's role and its effectiveness as an anti-fraud measure.

Internal audit

Internal audit in the detection of fraud is described in more detail in Chapter 4. In the context of addressing fraud risk, internal audit has the task of helping to improve the performance of controls, risk management and governance processes across the organisation. According to the Institute of Internal Auditors, "Internal auditors should have sufficient knowledge to identify indicators of fraud, but they are not expected to have the expertise of a person whose prime responsibility is preventing and detecting fraud." The internal auditor typically reports to the audit committee and, in turn, to the external auditor.

Having said this, internal audit is increasingly expected to play a larger part in controlling fraud risk. Very often, internal auditors are called upon to investigate incidents and allegations of fraud as they arise. Internal audit is also likely to be responsible for investigating, on behalf of the audit committee, allegations of fraud that are raised via the whistleblower hotline. As the range of responsibilities expands, there will be an ever greater need to equip internal audit teams with the anti-fraud and investigative skills that are increasingly demanded of them.

All employees

There are many roles within the organisation that have a clearly defined responsibility in relation to dealing with fraud risk. However, the vast majority within the organisation have no such defined responsibilities but without the attention, cooperation and diligence of the entire workforce, it would be impossible adequately to confront the risk of fraud.

As we will explain later in Chapter 4, employee tip-offs have historically played a very significant role in uncovering frauds and unethical practice. This means that employees need to be provided with an environment in which they feel compelled to act appropriately and operate controls, and sufficiently empowered to speak up or challenge where they see misconduct in whatever form.

So, whilst they represent the largest proportion of the organisation's people, their effectiveness in the management of fraud risk is critically dependent upon the example set by leadership in the way that they execute their responsibilities. If expectations are clear and the ethical tone is unambiguous, there is a far greater chance that anti-fraud measures will be effective.

Trust – the essential element

All fraud risk management activities are also built upon the trust that pervades the organisation. Trust in fellow colleagues and business partners is one element of a business and managerial culture that works well in facilitating operations. It recognises the strong 'human element' in negotiations that works without formal and controlled arrangements. But the culture of trust also needs sanctions for those that would abuse it. When problems arise, the task of unpicking the trust will be painful. A trusted individual may create a sort of cocoon around himself, which senior management are unable to penetrate. They may be very successful but almost untouchable. Trusted individuals are often high flyers in very specialist areas overseen by management who are not close to the detail and "leave the individuals alone" as long as they are delivering results.

The trust culture risks distracting management from an objective interpretation of warning signs, as was the case with Nick Leeson. Even though he was apparently producing market leading results, trust may have prevented anyone in a senior position from asking the difficult questions.

The problem with the trusted relationship is not when it is working well, but when it starts to break down or, when something occurs that undermines management trust. People tend to disbelieve warning signs, on the basis that they do not have the capacity to challenge the individual, perhaps after a long period of trust-based neglect. Managers continue to avoid facing up to the problem because they find it too difficult to address – it means that they may have to admit to themselves that they have been wrong to place so much trust in the individual. The balance of power in such a relationship is often with the employee because they have been the top performers and have acquired the status that accompanies that. They need to be treated carefully so that they avoid feeling that they are being victimised. But often, the greatest risk to the organisation is realised by ignoring the warning signs for too long.

There is a dichotomy between trust and accountability. Organisations may not want to feel that they stifle creativity, by implementing complex processes rather than making sure people are accountable. This is a balance that is hard to get right.

The strains on a board that faces dealing with a top and trusted employee who is suspected of fraud or other abuses are severe. This is because the top trader or senior manager is likely to have built up around him a large and loyal network of supporters, and their loyalty to the company can no longer be assumed. Companies shy away from making the difficult decisions with regard to these individuals at their peril, as their positions mean that they have the potential to wreak considerable damage on their organisations.

Where action is taken some companies will automatically prosecute those found to be committing fraud, however small the fraud, to demonstrate a policy of zero tolerance. Some will name and shame employees found to be acting fraudulently to send out a deterrent.

One company executive said that when she had to bring the police into an investigation, she didn't always take them straight to her office. "I took them on the most indirect route, so that people could see that this was the action that we took when we had a problem. That in itself is part of how we manage fraud risk – deterance is better than detection."

---

1. http://lnadbg4.adb.org/oai001p.nsf/0/F77A326B818A19C548257853000C2B10/$FILE/cross-debarment-agreement.pdf

2. http://www.adb.org/site/integrity/news/articles-case-studies/after-cross-debarment-agreement

3. http://www.crossdebarment.org

4. *Guidance on Audit Committees*, Financial Reporting Council, September 2012

Chapter 3

What drives the fraudster?

Introduction

At a fundamental level, businesses are all about people. They are dynamic entities driven by the beliefs, actions and choices of individuals. Similarly, fraud is about people and the drivers and characteristics that cause them to feel and act in the way that they do.

Research by organisations that specialise in dealing with fraud risks, such as the Association of Certified Fraud Examiners (ACFE), and our own experience of investigating large scale fraud show that fraudsters are often 'ordinary' people who encountered circumstances which led them to take the first steps in committing a fraud. Even the largest frauds usually start on a small scale and grow over time. As the Chairman of Satyam, Ramalinga Raju, who admitted to inflating revenues by over $1bn, wrote in his resignation letter, "It was like riding a tiger, not knowing how to get off without being eaten." We will return to the Satyam story in Chapter 8.

In investigating frauds, we see the conditions that made the organisation vulnerable to fraud and corruption. These 'red flags' can be integral aspects of how the organisation operates and treats and motivates its employees. But for every rule there is an exception – in some cases predatory fraudsters select and target organisations.

Robert Hunter, a partner at Herbert Smith Freehills who, as an investigator, has encountered many of the highest-profile fraudsters in recent times, shares his perspective: "Most of the persistent fraudsters who seek out opportunities to deceive or betray over a long period of time are psychopathic personalities." Defining psychopathic traits include an individual's inability to feel guilt, remorse or empathy for others who are affected by their actions.

Extraordinary fraudsters, extraordinary frauds

In the past decades we have seen fraud cases involving the loss of billions of dollars. Some truly enormous frauds have hit the headlines. In the UK, the events at Guinness, Polly Peck, Barings Bank and Maxwell Communication Corporation gripped the nation as the stories unfolded on the front pages of the national press. Elsewhere, Enron, Worldcom, Satyam, Parmalat and Madoff have become shorthand for billion dollar frauds that destroyed or endangered organisations and livelihoods. Are there lessons that can be drawn to help organisations to protect themselves from such destructive individuals?

For the purposes of our assessment, it is significant that, without exception, each of these extraordinary events was associated with individuals who were larger than life characters often brought to public attention by the frauds that they perpetrated. Are there common characteristics that we see in these people that we should be looking for – and do their stories point to better ways to protect organisations from their malign influence? To assist our analysis, we have divided them into groups according to their characteristics.

- **Dominant leaders**, such as Bernie Ebbers (Worldcom) and Kenneth Lay (Enron), who managed to gain control of their organisations and perpetrated frauds that led to corporate collapse.

- **Flamboyant entrepreneurs** and their families, such as the Rajus (Satyam), the Maxwells or Calisto Tanzi (Parmalat), who created global only to destroy them as they eventually over-extended themselves and turned to fraud to sustain the illusion of success.

- **Charismatic people**, such as Bernard Madoff, Allen Stanford (convicted for fraud for his role in the Stanford Financial Group scandal) or Peter Clowes, (who, as explained further in chapter 6, defrauded thousands of British public sector workers of their savings) who constructed entire organisations which seemed to be just vehicles for perpetrating fraud on a massive scale.

- **Rogue employees**, often financial traders, such as Nick Leeson (Barings) and Jérôme Kerviel (Société Générale), who gained such an intimate understanding of the levers and controls of the organisations in which they worked that they could circumvent every protective measure to trade themselves into hugely loss-making positions. Eventually, Leeson caused the demise of Barings as an independent entity.

The prominent attributes associated with these individuals could also have a positive, potentially transformative, impact on organisations if channelled towards 'doing the right thing'.

Attribute	Positive outcome	Negative outcome
Use of position to achieve things that others cannot	Implements fundamental change through clear and decisive action	Takes actions in their own interests rather than, or in spite of, those of the organisation
Intelligent, with a strong understanding of accounting processes and systems	Clear appreciation of the financial impact of their strategic decisions	Exploits control weakness to execute transactions which are then hidden within complex accounting constructs
Strong ego and great confidence	Conviction in their actions inspires confidence in others	Certainty that they will not be detected or, if they are, that they would be able to 'talk their way out of it'
Strong and persuasive personality	Inspires employees to perform above their potential	Cajoles individuals either to execute or ignore inappropriate activities
Powerful and credible communicator	Able to disguise any self doubts which might undermine the organisation	Excellent liar – able to convince colleagues, regulators and auditors
Resistant to the effects of pressure	Makes important decisions with conviction, despite conflicting demands	Copes with the stress of performing and then hiding a fraud

So here is the great challenge for those seeking to 'spot' a fraudster. If you can detect the tell-tale sociopathic or psychopathic tendencies, it may be possible to keep the extreme individuals outside your organisation. But personal traits and characteristics are so complex that those of the most successful and inspirational leaders can be almost indistinguishable from the most audacious fraudsters. And perhaps it is precisely because these fraudsters were believed, trusted and often even admired and acclaimed for their leadership that their frauds went undetected for so long.

Profiling the 'ordinary' fraudster

Perhaps the exception in our analysis of these notorious fraudsters is Leeson. He caused massive losses to his organisations but, unlike the others, the frauds that he instigated seemed to define him rather than the other way around. What can we see in these and similar 'rogue' individuals that sets them apart from the honest employee? Is there some way to characterise the 'ordinary' fraudster?

There has been a great deal of research on the attributes and drivers that explain why an individual commits fraud. These studies, which inevitably can only be undertaken in relation to known incidents of fraud, are nevertheless empirical in nature which means that they have value in identifying the risk factors.

The first group of studies are those that examine the social and educational backgrounds of known fraudsters. These have been undertaken by organisations such as the ACFE and the big four accountancy firms. The most recent ACFE Report to the Nations on Occupational Fraud and Abuse (RTTN), published in 2012[1], presents a rich array of such statistics. This document is publicly available and the reference is noted at the end of this chapter. We have selected a few of the findings to illustrate the results of the research in terms of four dimensions.

- **Age.** Looking at five-year ranges of age, the ACFE found that the most prolific group was in the range 41 to 45. They also discovered that more than half of frauds analysed were committed by those in the range 31 to 45. The research showed that the older the perpetrator, the greater the magnitude of the damage to the organisation.

- **Tenure.** A little more than one in 20 frauds was committed by individuals with less than one year of service. This compares with the observation that those whose tenure was between one and five years committed a little over 40% of the frauds. Even allowing for the longer period that this covers, it represents a significant increase. Inevitably, perhaps, the magnitude of losses associated with fraud incidents increases with tenure as the perpetrators accrue greater knowledge, access and trust.

- **Gender.** Overall, approximately two-thirds of frauds within the study were committed by men. The proportion varied by region: in North America, it fell to around half, whereas in the rest of the world, it was up to four-fifths. More significantly, the study established that frauds committed by men on average resulted in losses that were higher than those committed by women, a finding that was consistent at each level of the organisation.

- **Education.** The researchers found that just over half of fraudsters held a university degree or higher qualification. The higher the level of qualification, the greater the value of the losses associated with the fraud.

Stepping back from these statistics, we consider that the findings are not particuarly surprising. A fraudster is more likely to be well educated, to have been at the company for at least a year, to be between 31 and 45 and to be male – these are the same people who know the systems and have the required level of access, trust and experience to exploit them. A range of other surveys have provided a consistent perspective of the typical fraudster – male, in middle management, perhaps in his thirties and who has been with the organisation for around five years. Looking forward, as the proportion of women in senior positions increases, it is possible that the 'gender gap' will also narrow.

Unfortunately, and perhaps unsurprisingly, this is also the profile of a large proportion of an organisation's employees; indeed, looking around any organisation, we would see many individuals who fit the profile. So, does this mean that fraudsters have a perfect disguise? Do they simply hide in plain sight, only revealing themselves when it is too late? Or are there other ways of seeing what is right before our eyes?

The Fraud Triangle

To explore this further, we turn to a related perspective on the nature of the fraudster and what drives him – the Fraud Triangle. This empirical model was developed in the 1950s by Donald Cressey[2] and remains a widely recognised predictive model for the prerequisites of fraudulent activity. There is a significant body of literature in relation to this model so we will not provide a full analysis here. However, for the purposes of identifying the circumstances in which fraud is more likely to take place, it is worth considering the elements of the model: motivation, opportunity and rationalisation.

The 'motivation' to commit a fraud can arise from a variety of sources. It could perhaps stem from the need to obtain funds to maintain a certain quality of life or, in times of recession, to save the jobs of a loyal workforce who have become more like family.

Added to this motivation is the 'opportunity'; the opportunity for the would-be fraudster to make the changes, decisions or transactions necessary to achieve his aims. Perhaps opportunity is presented by a preventative control that does not work properly or a board which places such trust in one individual that he is able to bypass every control and make entirely autonomous decisions.

The final side of the triangle is 'rationalisation'. To some observers, this is the key element although it is the most difficult to identify. Motivation and opportunity present themselves to employees on a regular basis without leading to an act of fraud. The 'ordinary' fraudster needs to be able to believe that he has a justifiable reason for committing fraud. Perhaps it is a conviction that that no one is being harmed, that he somehow deserves the rewards or that he is simply 'borrowing' the money to pay it back at a later date.

Many observers note that this final point is useful in considering the likely actions of the majority of employees. This is illustrated further by the

ACFE's 'workplace deviance model'[3]. This suggests that only 10% of employees can be relied upon to be 'totally honest', while as many as 10% might be described as 'totally dishonest' – in other words, irrespective of rationalisation, the former will never commit fraud, whilst the latter will always do so if the opportunity presents itself. The corollary of this is that the vast majority of the workforce (that is the 80% in the middle ground) is capable of being influenced to behave either well or badly, and can rationalise in either direction depending on the nature of the external and internal forces. This provides an opportunity for directors and managers to reduce fraud risk by strengthening internal controls within the organisation. But, by the same token, this suggests that some 90% of all employees are, under the right circumstances, capable of fraud and dishonesty.

Recently, researchers, commentators and fraud investigators have started to refine the concepts of the Fraud Triangle approach. For example, in their research paper 'The New Fraud Triangle Model'[4], Rasha Kassem and Andrew Higson present an assessment of the merits of the various approaches that have emerged where other factors, particular that of 'capability', are seen to be a significant factor. Which can be seen to create a 'fraud diamond'.

Considerations around capability may be seen as helping to address the challenge of identifying the 'ordinary' fraudster[5]. They identified four capability-related traits which have the merit of being potentially observable from outside:

1. These people hold some form of authoritative position or function within the organisation.

2. They have the capacity to understand accounting systems and internal controls.

3. They are confident that detection is unlikely or, if caught, can be explained away.

4. They are able to deal with the stress of deception.

These are not significantly different from those attributes of the 'extraordinary' fraudster that we described earlier, so perhaps we are seeing a degree of consistency and the emergence of a potentially reliable set of risk factors which could be detectable.

Whichever model we use, however, the fact remains that an organisation cannot wholly rely on spotting the confluence of three (or four) factors to distinguish the critical risk of a fraud, simply because these factors are so hard to recognise at a sufficiently early stage. There is no 'silver bullet' technique for independently assessing when an employee is on the verge of committing a fraud.

The value of these models is, however, in informing the design of anti-fraud programmes and conducting fraud risk assessments. These models point to the likely existence of a 'tipping point' when all factors align to make a fraud possible. We now turn to considering the characteristics of organisations which are at greater risk of being the victims of fraud and in which employees are balanced on the verge of such a tipping point.

Dominant values – playing the corporate trump card

There are typically a number of imperatives that drive the behaviours of an individual or a business. We can classify these imperatives as positive or negative when considering their influence on an employee at the tipping point of committing fraud. Objectives that solely value short-term gains, perpetual sales growth or profit margin targets at any cost are likely to result in behaviours that are one-dimensional and, in the context of our potential fraudster, higher risk. This will be magnified in times when economic forces or other external factors conspire against the achievement of such goals.

We could also conclude that the CEO, encouraged and rewarded to expand the corporation through aggressive acquisitions, may find himself in a situation where he chooses to present an exaggerated view of his success. In this case, his capabilities and characteristics are turned against the interests of the company's shareholders or wider society through a distortion of the company's key values.

This distortion of an organisation's values is akin to playing the corporate equivalent of the trump card – an overriding justification for any activity that achieves the perceived aims of the organisation, even if that activity is fraudulent. This may be part of the explanation for the gene-sis of Bernard Madoff's behaviour. His early investors were family and friends to whom he had promised a particularly high rate of return. Such a situation, the combination of a single, principal trump card of high rates of return with the pressures associated with having made promises to individuals so close to him, placed him on the verge of the 'tipping point' from the very start.

At the other extreme, we see organisations that explicitly set out to create a much more benevolent culture. The Body Shop was founded by the late Dame Anita Roddick, a renowned human rights activist. The company still displays messages that are consistent with her beliefs as shown throughout its website. On one page, titled 'Our Company' is the statement "The business of business should not just be about money, it should be about responsibility. It should be about public good, not private greed." Imagine an individual in the situation where a number of factors and motivations are aligned to put him on the verge of fraudulent activity. In an organisation that can so openly declare a broader, longer-term set of values, such an individual may be less likely to step over the edge.

This all leads to the conclusion that in order to have a chance of preventing the employee from stepping over the edge, the organisation needs to have a set of pervasive values that promote a balanced set of objectives. These need to promote success not just in terms of profitability and growth, but also in terms of longer-term objectives such as stability and integrity.

But does such a positive set of values truly protect an organisation from the risk of rogue employees and the damage that they can inflict? Is there any way in which even what seem to be overwhelmingly positive values may be distorted to create an unexpected trump card that would justify inappropriate behaviour? In our view this illustrates a potential problem with values that may be considered extreme or idealistic. Perhaps an organisation that is outspokenly dedicated to the welfare of its employees above all else will create a situation where a rogue employee, subject to a combination of pressures that include the threat of a branch or division closure, may decide that an act of fraud is the only thing that will save the day. In such a situation, the trump card played is the 'honourable' intention of saving jobs.

It is therefore worth considering the values of every organisation that we encounter. Do they promote a balanced set of values that avoid the extremes? Or does one imperative, no matter how apparently positive, dominate to such an extent that it could become the trump card deployed in a time of personal or corporate crisis to justify questionable behaviours?

Rules are made to be broken

How does an organisation create a balanced set of values? One approach is to start with the understanding that rigid objectives and rules can turn against the organisation. Companies which favour prescriptive rules over principles-based approaches to conducting their business face significant challenges in ensuring ethical behaviour among their employees.

Rules can be too specific and too limited to a narrow set of circumstances. By making it clear what precisely should (or should not be) done in a particular eventuality, a business needs to be able to anticipate all possible eventualities. In the event that a scenario has not been considered, it becomes hard for an employee to know what rule to apply and how. Frequently, this encourages the creation of 'workarounds' in much the same way that overly complex tax legislation can create more opportunities to find loopholes than it prevents.

Principles, on the other hand, are more widely applicable and, if sensibly formulated, make clear an employee's appropriate path of action or the behaviour expected of them. Dee Hock, founder and former CEO of the Visa credit card association, stated: "Simple, clear purposes and principles give rise to complex and intelligent behaviour. Complex rules and regulations give rise to simple and stupid behaviour."[6] This suggests, therefore, that to create a balanced set of values, organisations should seek to frame these as overarching principles rather than more tightly defined targets.

Structural factors

As a final consideration, the structure of a business can result in conditions more or less prone to inappropriate conduct. We have seen the various factors that lead to an increase in fraud risk. A top-down, hierarchical structure is likely to promote the kind of powerful, dominating leadership that, unchecked, has become associated with many of the highest-profile frauds.

Similarly, the extent to which values permeate through the organisation may be heavily influenced by the way in which the organisation has grown. Those that have achieved organic growth are more likely to be based on a consistent set of values which are shared by individuals who consider themselves to be part of the success. Growth through acquisition may bring together organisations that have very different values. Neither of these may be inappropriate, but the existence in the latter of two differing approaches may bring conflict and confusion.

Finally, the importance of building a strong and consistent message that pervades an entire organisation is illustrated by considering the differing challenges presented by organisations that operate in a centralised way, as compared with those that are more decentralised. The further away from the 'centre' an employee stands, the less likely it is that such messages will resonate with clarity. It is worth considering whether that is the case in your organisation; can you be sure that those in remote locations understand and care about those values espoused at the centre? When push comes to shove, and the pressures and temptations mount, could this mean that the wavering employee is more likely to turn towards fraud and deception?

1. http://www.acfe.com/uploadedfiles/ACFE_Website/Content/rttn/2012-report-to-nations.pdf

2. Cressey, D. R. (1950) 'The criminal violation of financial trust'. *American Sociological Review* Vol. 15, No. 6 (December), pp. 738–743

3. Giles, S. (2012) *Managing fraud risk: A guide for directors and managers*

4. *Journal of Emerging Trends in Economics and Management Sciences* (JETEMS) 3(3), pp. 191–195.

5. Wolfe, D. T. and D. R. Hermanson, (2004) 'The fraud diamond: Considering the four elements of fraud.' *The CPA Journal*, December, pp. 1–5.

6. Dee Hock (1994) http://www.entheos.com/quotes/by_teacher/Dee%20Hock

Chapter 4

Fraud detection: Building the intelligent company to stay ahead of fraud

Introduction

In 1995, Nick Leeson lost £862m betting on the financial markets and brought down Britain's oldest investment bank. He later claimed that "it all started when I tried to cover for a junior colleague who had lost £20,000". As this and other cases show, massive frauds often start out as relatively small frauds. Detecting the signs when the fraud is still 'small' is not easy. It requires concerted effort and the fostering of an ethical corporate culture in which people will notice and then speak up when they see the early fraud signs – an environment in which the pressure of short-term goals does not override ethical principles.

The early detection of fraud will save money, but it is often the reputational damage associated with fraud and corruption that brings down organisations, as customers, suppliers, employees and investors disassociate themselves from the tainted brand. Earlier detection will give the organisation a better chance of protecting its reputation before the damage is irreparable.

Every fraud – from the overstated expense claim all the way to the manipulated financial statements and fraudulent market announcements which can ultimately lead to the demise of organisations – leaves an information trail. The challenge is to uncover the traces of this information trail before the losses become too damaging; to hear the corporate equivalent of the alarm bell. This period between the initiation of a fraud and its eventual discovery can be defined as the 'exposure gap' – the time in which the organisation is left open to ever-increasing losses.

This is not simply an academic argument; history is littered with rogues who conducted huge frauds for years without detection. With the luxury of hindsight, we can see that during such periods, there were patterns and suspicions either not noticed or not pieced together to raise the alarm. The American currency trader, John Rusnak, was able to defraud AIB of $691m over the course of five years before being detected. Even more dramatically, the Ponzi scheme, which Bernard Madoff used to defraud investors of $65bn, may have been in operation for more than 40 years. The ACFE's RTTN reports that the average fraud lasts 18 months from initiation to detection.

The early discovery of the fraud information trail and the corresponding narrowing of the exposure gap require elements of the following to be in place:

1. An environment where employees and others are motivated to report their concerns.

2. A review framework, which includes regular audits that look for indicators of fraud and other misconduct.

3. A monitoring capability, which includes automated analysis of transactions and the identification of patterns of unusual activity.

In this chapter, we will discuss each of these in turn. We will explain in more detail how we have seen leading organisations create an effective and trusted whistleblower framework. This is complemented by an independent and empowered internal audit function, and forensic data analytics which helps to identify the unusual 'needles in the haystack'.

The value of an investment in fraud detection and deterrence systems is demonstrated when a company successfully closes the 'exposure gap'. By identifying frauds more quickly, it is not only able to staunch further losses but also to have a greater chance of recovering funds before they are dissipated and of limiting reputational damage. Such a capacity is of particular importance in today's difficult economic environment, when anti-fraud budgets are under pressure just as the risk of fraud is heightened.

Measures to detect fraud operate at different levels and with varying degrees of effectiveness. The increasing use of automated analysis of transactions for businesses, forensic data analytics enables businesses to build the bigger picture of their business activity, and what would fall outside of the 'norm'. Picking up those deviations can be the key to uncovering a fraud just as it's starting. Internal controls can be, and often are, overridden by people. Automated analysis cannot. This type of reporting should go hand in hand with the encouragement of whistleblowers to report concerns and internal audits as a first defence barrier.

Employees are your eyes and ears for spotting fraud

Dealing with internal information

The ACFE's RTTN concluded that three times as many frauds are discovered by tip-off than by any other method. A senior investigator confirms this by citing a fraud by a purchasing clerk. "The people most likely to pick up the red flags are those who are sitting in the immediate area of the fraudster. The accounts clerk in a major procurement fraud case did precisely that. He used to watch his boss go and get his [fraudulent] invoices approved."

Beyond more effective detection, the impact of a whistleblower hotline on the discovery and investigation of fraud is highlighted in the RTTN. There, the ACFE reported that companies with fraud hotlines experience smaller fraud losses, and that the average exposure gap between the start of a fraud and its eventual discovery is reduced by seven months. As a further benefit, the disclosure of such complaints internally gives the company the chance to keep control of the investigation and to have a greater chance of managing the subsequent news agenda.

Responding to reports from whistleblowing hotlines is often the most effective way to really help companies prevent fraud. Based on our experience, on average, one out of 20 reports is likely to have a substantial fraud allegation that requires follow up.

When information comes from an unexpected source

Whilst employees are clearly a good source of information, other stakeholders also see things to which the organisation is blind. In one case, a Scandinavian company which had repeatedly failed to win any business from a construction company in Africa, wrote to the construction company's private equity owners to report its suspicions of corruption. The Scandinavian company had 'tested' the system by placing one bid at a deliberately low price but had still failed to win any business.

Investigations revealed that the manager of the construction company routinely awarded contracts to a small group of suppliers which were connected to him and his family through shared ownership.

If whistleblowers are the first line of detection, how do organisations encourage people to speak out, and what are the barriers to such a valuable channel of information? In theory, the answer is simple – provide a practical mechanism and address the concerns that prevent people from speaking up. In practice, it takes time and direction from the very senior levels of the organisation to create such an environment.

Employees will be motivated to report suspicions of wrongdoing by colleagues and outsiders in organisations when there is a culture of transparency and compliance. But personal factors, such as loyalties or fear of retaliation, will ultimately determine whether an individual will speak up. Employees who spot a fraud will face many conflicts and anxieties: do they make their own enquiries of the person they suspect; do they report it to a manager; do they share it with colleagues; do they report it through a whistleblowing hotline; do they turn a blind eye and pretend nothing is happening?

Fraudsters who are confronted may also become defensive, potentially seeking to recruit the colleague who has approached them. This will particularly be the case if the fraudster thinks that the person can be trusted to share in the benefits in exchange for keeping quiet. Alternatively, he may also threaten to damage the whistleblower's career, if he is in a position to do so.

The position of a junior executive suspecting fraud at a senior level (even the board) is a particularly precarious one, as the senior manager may seek to pull rank, arguing he has confidential knowledge which justifies his suspicious behaviour. The senior employee who sees his fraudulent scheme challenged may threaten the junior colleague's position in the company, his promotion prospects or his bonus.

The solution lies in dealing with the personal and professional risks that employees see in whistleblowing – obtaining an understanding of the tipping point at which employees decide to defy their feelings of fear and report suspicions of fraud. There may be a personal element: for example, the breakdown of the working relationship with the fraudster, which drives employees to finally report their suspicions. One investigator noted: "People sometimes pick up not on the fraud itself, but on the behaviour which underlies the fraudulent activity. For example, boasting about being able to 'work the systems'. In other cases, people have felt denied the opportunity for promotion and, as a result, become whistleblowers. People who fear their job may be at risk also have a motive to report a fraud, with the rationale that they will improve their chances of retaining their job as their loyalty will be rewarded."

A proactive way of breaking down the barriers to reporting is to train management on how to deal sensitively and fairly with whistleblowers. This is critical in securing the ongoing cooperation of the whistleblower and demonstrating that the company values ethical and honest behaviour at all levels.

Employees who bring a suspicion of fraud to a manager are likely to be extremely nervous and uncertain. They need to be handled professionally, and managers need to be prepared for this and know how to respond, otherwise reactions can vary from starting an investigation to seeking to suppress the report. In one case, a senior executive told a whistleblower, "Let's keep this quiet. We don't wash our dirty laundry in public." Establishing a whistleblowing hotline is one mechanism for establishing a confidential and secure channel for employees to report concerns.

Communicating the existence of a hotline and emphasising its importance is paramount. Employees need to have faith in the integrity of the hotline, which may be emphasised by engaging an independent third party to operate it. Employees also need to be clear about its value. One manager advised: "You need to keep reminding people. So it's no good just telling people once that we have a whistleblowing line, you need to have posters up in canteens and common places. When people turn their screens on in the morning, the start-up page includes the link to the hotline, 'If you've got a concern, ring this number'. It is a very important counter-fraud measure. Launch, remind and maintain – that's the key."

The message to employees is that the company takes whistleblowing reports seriously and deals with them as confidential information. Hotlines enforce the company's message of transparency and ethical values, and they are most likely to be effective where employees understand and identify their company's goals and standards. The challenge for the employee is the grey area in which there is suspicion of wrongdoing but, in the absence of 'proof', the employee is reluctant to stigmatise a colleague unfairly. A senior external auditor recounts her experience: "Some people find it hard to whistleblow. They have got their suspicions but they don't know the whole story. It's quite hard to whistle blow unless you have enough information. Invariably you don't know the whole thing. So you're only going to know the little bit and just think that it's a bit strange and not necessarily worthy of reporting."

Whistleblowing allegations also need to be tested for their accuracy; the anonymity of the source can sometimes provide a screen for malicious reporting. In one case, the whistleblower was found to be both providing reliable information but also to hold a grudge. The lead investigator said: "the whistleblower had got wind of the fraud, but could not get in on the action. It was not a question of ethics. If he had been included in the fraud he would have been happy, but the fact that he hadn't been included was his sole motivation." The investigator continued: "If you can't trust the individuals, you can't trust the evidence or your instincts. So understanding the motivations of both the person who is committing fraud, and of the person reporting it, are important."

In summary, there are six considerations when designing and operating a whistleblower hotline[1]. In each case, there must be clear and unequivocal support from the very top of the organisation:

1. Companies need to promote their whistleblowing hotlines and policies. The whistleblowing process should be outlined through a variety of media such as screensavers and frequently updated training sessions.

2. Companies need to affirm their commitment regularly to their whistleblowing policy, and assert clearly and categorically that reports are thoroughly investigated and outcomes are fair. They may also enable whistleblowers to track the progress of the investigation.

3. Companies need to emphasise that the whistleblowing policy is designed to maintain the company's ethics and standards; it is not a matter of 'telling tales' on colleagues.

4. The hotline should be flexible so it can accommodate anything from concerns and suspicions to firm evidence.

5. Whistleblowing hotlines need to facilitate confidential reporting and to maintain the anonymity of the informant.

6. Companies must also demonstrate that they will protect the identity of whistleblowers, and they will face neither dismissal nor any form of disciplinary action, retaliation or victimisation arising as a result of disclosures made in good faith.

This tendency for many to look the other way when they suspect that a fraud is in progress is also recognised by governments and regulators around the world. The leaders of the G20 group of countries have signed up to the principle of protection of whistleblowers as being of the highest priority. Related legislation is in place across the globe[2]. In the US, the Sarbanes–Oxley Act of 2002 (enacted as a response to major corporate scandals, including those at Enron and WorldCom) requires the audit committee to establish procedures for the confidential or anonymous submission by employees of concerns about questionable accounting practices. The UK Corporate Governance Code requires audit committees to "review arrangements by which staff of the company may raise concerns in confidence about possible improprieties."[3]

The reality is that whistleblowers can still suffer consequences in their personal and professional lives. In response, for example, the UK law regarding whistleblowers – the Public Interest Disclosure Act (PIDA) – gives whistleblowers added protection from reprisals by their employers, provided they are not acting in bad faith. However, there remain significant cultural and regional variations in attitudes towards whistleblowing.

Jack Blum, a US lawyer active in the regulatory field who spent 14 years as a senate investigator, cites the case of a company that closed down an internal auditor's investigation and stigmatised the whistleblower. "What stiffens the back of internal auditors is when there are regulators who are on the job and say, you can't do that kind of thing or we'll come after you. Unless the regulators are on the beat and doing what they're supposed to be doing, people will not make disclosures as no one wants to acquire a reputation as a whistleblower and a troublemaker. That is where the internal controls break down."

In the UK, new bribery legislation brings a different kind of motivation to organisations. This legislation includes a 'strict liability' offence, where the only defence is having 'adequate procedures' within the company designed to prevent corrupt activity. Such procedures are expected to include the provision of a whistleblower hotline.

The emergence of this legislation represents enormous risks for the corporate that seeks to bury a matter of concern once it has been detected. Where a suspicion of fraud or corruption is brought to the attention of a regulator or other authority through a whistleblower after the company has sought to ignore it or failed to detect it, it will add to the company's ultimate exposure.

The growing international consensus gives Arpinder Singh, FIDS Leader at EY in India, grounds for optimism. "If hotlines became mandatory in every country, how things will change! Companies will no longer take a chance of not doing an investigation, because they know it is a matter of time. It is a ticking time bomb. Educated people will be well aware of the hotline concept. They know that if the company wants to try and bury the issue, they have the option to go to the local regulators, or the foreign regulators where the company is based overseas, and to blow the whistle. They may choose to leak information to the media."

While the sense of responsibility is clearly a very strong impetus to report a problem, and legal protection helps further, regulators have demonstrated a belief that employees are even more likely to make a disclosure if there is a monetary incentive. This has resulted in a growing number of countries adopting legislation enabling whistleblowers to benefit personally if information they provide is instrumental to a successful investigation.

The US has led the way in adopting several pieces of legislation which provide whistle blowers with financial incentives. The most recent are the provisions in the Dodd-Frank Wall Street Reform and Consumer Protection Act (2010), which were enacted following the banking industry meltdown. Under these provisions, subject to certain limitations and conditions, a whistle blower who voluntarily provides the SEC with original information about a violation of the securities laws which leads to financial penalties exceeding $1m, can be personally be awarded between 10% and 30% of the amounts collected. This is a well-funded program - as at 30 September 2012, the fund established by the SEC to finance the whistleblower award program, had a balance of over $450m[4].

Other US legislation which provides financial incentives for whistleblowers includes the Tax Relief and Healthcare Act of 2006 and the False Claims Act which dates back to the US civil war. The former provides for incentives of up to 30% of the additional tax and penalties collected as a result of a report. The False Claims Act relates to instances in which the United States government has been defrauded. Whistleblower rewards paid under this legislation have historically been significant. For example, in 2010, the US government paid Cheryl Eckard, a former quality assurance manager at a pharmaceutical company, $96m under the False Claims Act for exposing production deficiencies. However, whistleblower financial incentive schemes are not limited to the United States and are being adopted in many jurisdictions, such as the UK where the Office of Fair Trading offers financial rewards for reports relating to anti-competitive practices.

The implication for businesses is that whistleblowers could be encouraged to bypass internal mechanisms and make reports directly to the regulators - despite some regulators' guidance to the contrary. Some companies are already considering fighting regulator payouts with their own financial incentives. Most companies have responded by reinforcing their communication on the use of internal whistleblowing mechanisms, using forensic data analytics to identify indicators of fraud and corruption, and interviewing departing employees on whether they are aware of any wrongdoing.

Making sure your whistleblowing hotline rings

1. Establish and publicise a hotline and, when information comes in, treat it seriously, even if the allegations seem unlikely.

2. Insist on employees disclosing relationships with suppliers and customers. Ensure that those stakeholders also understand the whistleblowing framework.

3. Conglomerates need well-monitored channels for disclosure between subsidiaries and headquarters.

Management solutions to an information deficit

Internal audit

A second component of the detection process is the existence of a strong, independent and effective internal audit function. There are a number of important elements of such a function, and these are covered in the following section.

The task of addressing the risk of fraud and misconduct across an organisation typically falls, at least in part, to the internal audit function. This requires a combination of tact, diplomacy and robustness when challenging the conduct or professionalism of senior managers. The regular and visible assessment of each department's control systems and processes sends out a powerful and valuable deterrence message that should bolster an appropriate tone set by the organisation's leadership. If senior members of the organisation can be subject to scrutiny and audit, then no one is 'above the law'.

Surprise intenal audits

Regular internal audits are aimed at ensuring either process control, adherence to policy or regulatory compliance. Managers are given notice and are expected to prepare themselves and their teams to respond to auditors' enquiries. This form of scrutiny and assessment is focused more on procedural compliance than on wrongdoing, and is part of the regulatory and internal control arrangements of a business.

But the surprise audit has a completely different purpose, aimed as it is at intercepting arrangements or plans that are not part of a manager's disclosed or legitimate activities. These audits can stop fraudulent or inefficient practices in their tracks. It gives the audit committee a truer view into the operation of departments and puts would-be fraudsters on notice.

Surprise audits are relatively rare in companies but tend to be most common in businesses where cash and stock move fast. Managers who have something to hide, whether it be poor or inefficient working arrangements or fraud, will be able to prepare a better picture of their performance when the audit is prearranged than when auditors arrive unexpectedly.

Introducing an element of surprise has long been an effective management technique for ensuring that businesses are operating in line with expectations. However, many of the benefits of a 'surprise audit' can be achieved simply by taking a less rigid approach to auditing. This may include providing information requests at relatively short notice, undertaking data analysis during the planning stages to focus the fieldwork on areas of higher risk or empowering the audit field team to make tactical decisions in terms of areas of review whilst they are on the ground.

When planning the audit strategy, auditors need to make an assessment of fraud risk by looking for factors that either increase or mitigate such a risk. One senior audit partner identifies some of the 'red flags' associated with an elevated risk of fraud to be as follows:

1. A bullying CEO will surround himself with weak characters. The finance function may be under-resourced and the finance team members will often be quite weak but perhaps overpaid for what they do. This is a risk factor as management override is a feature common to many of the most significant corporate frauds that have emerged in recent years.

2. A firm that uses unknown professional advisers attracts immediate attention. Advisers should be of good reputation or proven track record and, most importantly, they should want to do the right thing. As a senior audit partner puts it, "You'd think it rather odd if they are dealing with a law firm that you had never heard of. You ask yourself, 'Are they getting the right advice from the right sort of people or are they trying to do it on the cheap or for some other reason?'."

3. A company that is disorganised also causes concern. The audit partner explains further, "I look at how well the company deals with deadlines. In a well-organised company, there are proper processes, proper governance and proper working papers."

4. Leaving difficult issues to the last minute in the course of an audit may be an indicator of increased fraud risk. In creating such circumstances, the company directors may be hoping that the auditor will wave through the problems without sufficient scrutiny to ensure a reporting deadline is achieved.

Configuring internal audit for detection

1. Establish an independent and credible internal audit function and provide them with the resources to fulfil their mandate.

2. Encourage them to adopt a range of strategies to increase their effectiveness in addressing fraud risk.

3. Ensure that they have real, visible support from senior management so that they have the credibility to challenge powerful people within the organisation.

Forensic data analytics

The third member of our trinity of detection strategies is automated analysis of business data to identify the 'unusual'. The first two strategies are dependent upon human factors, namely the encouragement of employees to make use of whistleblowing facilities and the expectation that an internal auditor will spot something that does not appear to be bona fide. Forensic data analytics brings a different factor to bear – that of machine-driven detection. When harnessed properly, this powerful approach can significantly tip the odds in favour of detecting a fraud much earlier in its life cycle, and thereby close the exposure gap. Forensic data analytics removes the people from the process and enables the machine to ask the right questions. Get this right, and the needle in the haystack will find itself.

Forensic data analytics as a means of detecting fraud starts with the premise that the tell-tale signs of fraud are to be found in the vast and rapidly growing amounts of data recorded and stored within the systems of companies and governments. The identification and interpretation of patterns that can be found in this information can point to characteristics of relationships or behaviours which may be indicative of wrongdoing. In the same way that humans will look for red flags in terms of individual behaviours or circumstances, forensic data analytics is used to identify red flags within the data. Forensic data analytics provides the opportunity to assess all of the information and, as we will discuss, start to identify new and emerging fraud schemes in addition to those schemes that have been seen before.

The challenge for the organisation in deploying forensic data analytics is three-fold: first, defining the questions that need to be asked of the data; second, identifying and then acquiring the data that is required for the analysis and third, selecting and utilising the many tools and techniques that are available to undertake that analysis. Each of these is challenging in itself – and each is the subject of a great deal of research. The purpose of this section is to provide an overview of each element of the process and to illustrate the ways in which they help to detect different types of fraudulent behaviour. Before describing the various elements, it is important to understand some of the terminology that is the lingua franca of this discipline.

Data is often divided into two classes – structured and unstructured. Structured data is held within the databases which underpin an organisation's day-to-day activity. Where fraud detection within corporate environments is concerned, this data most commonly takes the form of accounting data including, for example, general ledger journals or sales, purchases and cash transactions. Structured data can also be found within HR, marketing and other operational systems with the key features being that the data tends to be well defined, ordered and, generally, accessible.

Data can also reside in unstructured form. Traditionally, this has included emails, documents and presentations, but increasingly it is dominated by sources such as instant messages, websites, blogs, voice recordings and even pictures.

Naturally, there is middle ground which is often referred to as semi-structured; data which contains elements of each of the two ends. An example is workflow systems (such as procurement platforms) which provide a structure in which documents, free-text and even document images can be housed.

The respective ends of the scales pose very different challenges. The objective of the analysis of structured data may be seen in terms of the need to identify patterns and pictures hidden within the data. In contrast, the challenge with unstructured data is often described in terms of the need to bring enough order to facilitate the application of data analysis techniques.

Unstructured data is said to account for 80% of a typical company's total data assets. Furthermore, the amount of data in a company is doubling every two years. In a world in which the analysis of 'Big Data' is providing companies with significant competitive advantage this data must be seen as a rich source of anti-fraud intelligence for those with the skills and tools to exploit it[5].

A further class of unstructured data is found outside of the organisation – within the Internet. This includes sources which contain intelligence that may be relevant to the detection process, including blogs, online publications and other online repositories. Very often, the early signs of fraud or abuse appear in such forms as these are places where people are often at their most unguarded – sharing their concerns with others in their network or simply revealing their more personal thoughts to the world.

In response, an emerging class of tools and techniques is developing to detect the warning signs before the issues are picked up by the organisation's systems. This might include monitoring for an uptick in consumer complaints which, perhaps, conflicts with the underlying picture portrayed by reported transactions and balances. This is a new and fast-moving area, and more detailed discussion is outside the scope of this book.

Defining the questions: rules and models

Data analysis approaches can be described in terms of rules-based testing and model-based analysis. This distinction may be explained by reference to the diagram set out below.

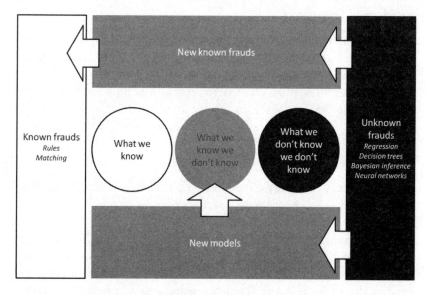

Figure 4.1 The relationship between rules and models

The usual (and most accessible) first steps in using data analysis to detect fraud is to focus on existing fraud schemes – the 'what we know'. The associated analysis is often described as 'rules' and 'matching' testing, as it is used to compare transactions and relationships with defined facts or patterns.

To use a simple example, in a number of high profile cases, bribes have been paid through offshore bank accounts. A rule to detect this would be to search the vendor master lists for those suppliers which bank in a defined set of high-risk offshore locations. Such rules can be relatively blunt in their application – there could be perfectly legitimate circumstances where a supplier holds bank accounts in such locations – and so such rules are prone to the identification of false positives.

One technique for improving the effectiveness of rules-based testing is to combine a number of single-rule tests. To extend the bribery example, this might be achieved by adding a further requirement that, to be selected, the vendor with an *off*shore bank account must have an *on*shore mailing address. This may be further refined by adding more rules and perhaps by assigning greater weight to those factors which experience tells us represent stronger indicators of the behaviour that we are seeking to detect.

Rules and matching techniques effectively codify the experience of an investigator. In other words, these techniques are used to identify fraud schemes that have already been defined based on past experience. However, one of the most challenging features of fraud and fraudsters is their ability to evolve and reappear in unexpected areas, using an unexpected modus operandi. Techniques are therefore required to counter this evolution and to detect these emerging threats – the so-called known and unknown 'unknowns'.

One response is to deploy more advanced analytical techniques, which are derived from the science of statistics and customer intelligence. This is the world of model-based testing – supervised and unsupervised analytics. In this context, supervised techniques involve the analysis of data surrounding known instances of fraud. These techniques – logistic regression being a commonly used example – involve identifying the statistically most relevant (in other words, most predictive) factors which distinguish the fraudulent transactions. The resultant model, which is in effect a very sophisticated rule, may then be applied to the wider population of transactions, and those that appear most similar to the model are selected for review.

Unsupervised techniques are used where the analyst does not have the luxury of starting with a set of known fraud cases. Instead, statistical techniques are deployed to identify 'unusual' transactions or relationships on the premise that such outliers are potentially the result of fraudulent activity. In this way, the computer can be said to learn the patterns, heuristics or specific rules which are indicative of fraud. Such models, which may even be used to detect previously unknown fraud schemes, may then be deployed as better, more sophisticated and discriminate fraud detection rules.

There are many statistical techniques that have been deployed in this way, including Bayesian inference and decision trees. Although a detailed discussion of these is beyond the scope of this book, these approaches may be illustrated by considering their application to managing the threat of insider fraud within an organisation.

The threat from the inside

All too often the emphasis of news reports on fraud is on the external threat: the hackers, fraudsters and money launderers who exploit weak spots in an organisation's defences. However, the reality is that a significant fraud threat comes from employees – those individuals that have been allowed *inside* the organisation.

The changes brought on by the development of new e-business systems and processes means the propensity for insiders to commit fraud and financial crime – and the opportunities for them to do so – is increasing faster than an organisation's ability to police them. An increased corporate focus on rapid results, risk-taking and entrepreneurialism has, arguably, contributed to a more fraud-friendly environment. Technology too has become a double-edged sword. The speed, power, pervasiveness, mobility and anonymity which benefit today's business models also offer attractive opportunities to individuals who are intent on committing fraud, money laundering and other forms of inappropriate behaviour. They are aided by the side effects of business process re-engineering and other forms of organi-sational de-layering which have resulted in the removal of many checks and balances, not to mention an increasing dependence on contractors and outsourcing[6].

Detecting insider fraud

Those who perpetrate insider fraud know an organisation's systems and controls and how to get around them. These are long-term frauds, and many fraudsters are very ingenious: according to a 2005 study on the insider threat by the US Secret Service and CERT Coordination Center/SEI,[7] 39% of attacks used a 'sophisticated' method. Departments responsible for containing insider fraud tend to focus on prevention through training and awareness-raising and HR policy statements, as well as detailed reactive investigation of cases as they come to light.

Detecting insider fraud is rather like looking for a needle in a haystack. Fraudsters need to preserve the secrecy of their activities; they know the controls and how to bypass them, and they are often well versed in the investigative process and know how to hide any incriminating evidence. It is clear then, that a purely 'rules-based' approach is unlikely to be fully effective in such dynamic circumstances, although, as discussed above, it is a very positive place to start.

Transactional data generated by the many different electronic systems they encounter give evidence of their activity. It makes sense, therefore, to use forensic data analysis to explore these data sources to identify signs of potentially fraudulent activity.

Intelligent analysis engines based on advanced data warehouse and data mining technology (to store and analyse data respectively), take in transaction trails from key systems around the organisation such as financial systems, call centre records, telephones, building entry gates, web servers and print servers. Personnel records from HR and finance systems supplement this. The wider the range of sources, the better – very often, data from a single source will be internally consist-ent, and anomalies and deviations may only become exposed as external data is added to the mix.

Incoming data is then stored in a data warehouse in a format that (crucially) retains the patterns of behaviour and how these develop and change over a long period of time. This is achieved by focusing on events and points at which data changes, rather than the data itself. This is where the model-based analysis discussed earlier comes into play. To illustrate this, included below are two methods of analysis which may be used to detect anomalous patterns for further investigation.

The first uses techniques within the class of clustering analysis to identify groups of similar entities in data without starting with explicit, known assumptions; in other words, it is an unsupervised technique. Such techniques (for example, k-means clustering) could be used to examine the behaviour of employees by reference to a range of attributes. Once clusters have been identified, 'dimensional data' such as department, role or start date may be overlaid so that the picture becomes richer and unusual outliers become very visible.

A second technique is a hybrid mix of supermarket-style loyalty scoring and classic Bayesian statistics that score people when they exhibit certain forms of behaviour consistent with insider fraud behaviour (for example, accessing an unusual combination of systems or undertaking a unique range of tasks within a transaction chain). A discriminating analytical approach can identify behavioural traits.

These algorithms, known as 'unsupervised neural networks', work by being set loose on a huge amount of data in order to work out for themselves what is suspicious without having to refer to a checklist of rules. The output from these systems can then be turned into rule-based forms in order to identify anomalies and therefore potential frauds. This could include, for example, identifying an unusual combination of authorisations which matches to a known fraud, and then testing the entire transaction set to identify other such instances which match this rule.

Approaches to unstructured data

The analysis of unstructured data brings both challenges and opportunities. Its inherent lack of homogeneity means that many of the data analysis techniques routinely used on structured data are not immediately applicable. However, this does not mean that no value can be derived from such data sources – quite the opposite in fact; it just requires a little more effort.

A major class of techniques fall under the general classification of 'text mining'. These include entity extraction (the identification of proper nouns from within the text), phrase extraction, key word analysis and sentiment analysis. Such techniques are a powerful adjunct to the analysis of structured data, where the analyst can assess the consistency (or otherwise) of a transactions effect with the sentiment expressed in associated narratives or documents. Where inconsistency is identified, transactions may be flagged up for investigation.

An emerging application for this relates to the analysis of the behaviour of financial traders to detect patterns that may be indicative of 'rogue' behaviour. This involves the analysis of the incidence of high risk words, the sentiment of communications and the financial trades that are being executed in the midst of these communications. In this way, forensic data analytics can help to distinguish the trader who is operating in ways that are inconsistent with their peers, the market or their own established behaviour.

Lessons from the financial services industry
The financial services industry has traditionally led the way in deploying leading-edge data analytics to address the challenge of detecting and preventing fraud.

Detection of forms of credit abuse is also achievable with such forms of analysis. Credit abuse involves organised fraudsters making false statements on application forms in order to gain credit, which they have no intention of paying back. These criminals are increasingly manipulating the credit application process, and it is in response to such organised fraud that another class of techniques known as social network analysis (SNA) has been brought into play.

SNA (which, as its names suggests, developed through the analysis of the linkages between individuals) is now being used to make high-speed checks of credit applicants' details against pre-scored criminal networks during the live application process. It is also being applied in the 'back office', where existing customers are scored as they request additional credit facilities. Banks can therefore 'shut out' and decline any applications that appear to emanate from those networks.

Such data mining has been put into the context of artificial intelligence. "One of the most successful commercial applications of artificial intelligence to date has been in the banking industry where computers have been employed as fraud detectives. Much of the work was originally pioneered in the mid 1980s, when credit card fraud losses were reaching unacceptably high levels. Since then, they have been used in other domains including anti-money laundering and sanctions-related monitoring. Look inside any bank today and you will find some kind of computerised fraud detection system that takes in huge volumes of transaction data and looks for tell-tale patterns in the data in order to identify potential fraud cases worthy of further investigation."

These detection systems make use of a body of rules that define the way that fraudsters and money launderers typically carry out their activities. If the rules are triggered, the activity can be deemed 'suspicious' and worthy of further investigation. One of the more obvious examples of a suspicious activity rule is when a dormant account suddenly comes alive with a burst of spending at certain types of retail outlet, or where large deposits into an account are mirrored by sudden immediate withdrawals. These systems often look for any kind of deviation from the account's normal, historical profile. Appropriately designed and deployed rule-based systems can draw attention to those transaction patterns that possess the highest likelihood of being suspicious and are therefore most likely to pose a risk.

Many banks are now moving from end-of-day analysis to near realtime analysis as the transactions actually occur, to move from reactive fire-fighting to proactive prevention of financial loss and damage to reputation. The increase in efficiency and effectiveness of the detection process leads to cost savings and competitive advantage: the cost of fraud comes straight off the bottom line, and a small reduction in losses can result in considerable bottom-line growth. Reducing fraud can, in some cases, make the difference between a new financial services product being profitable or not.

Data mining for straitened times

Whilst many (although not all) of the analysis tools are relatively inexpensive, forensic data analytics represents a task that is usually undertaken by specialists. However, such expertise can be expensive so such an outlay needs to be justified – now even more than ever. Fraud detection can be shown to result in tangible cash benefits and, in some cases, even competitive advantage. This in itself can provide the positive return on investment demanded by most organisations. Beyond this, however, the fact that data is being used and manipulated in this way means that analysts generate insights that do not solely pertain to fraud detection. Experience has shown that this analysis generates insights that are valuable in themselves or point to areas of inefficiency or which waste, and therefore signpost opportunities to make savings.

Deployment of data analytics

1. Organisations do not need to start by using the most advanced analytics. The use of even the most rudimentary analysis will improve the chance of detecting fraud, and will start to build the organisation's confidence in its value.

2. Organisations should not be afraid of copying ideas from other industries or fields of analysis. The financial services sector leads the way in the use of data analytics for fraud risk management.

3. Analysis can generate a range of benefits beyond fraud detection. Using this to widen the range of advocates across the business will increase acceptance and the will to invest further.

1. Giles, S. (2012) *Managing fraud risk: A guide for directors and managers*

2. G20 Anti-Corruption Action Plan, Action Point 7: Protection of Whistleblowers (November 2010)

3. *Guidance on Audit Committees*, Financial Reporting Council 2012

4. U.S. Securities and Exchange Commission, Annual Report on the Dodd-Frank Whistleblower program, Fiscal Year 2012

5. Porter, David. (2009) 'The Complex New World of Information Security', taken from *Handbook of Research on Social and Organizational Liabilities in Information Security*. Information Science Reference

6. Porter, ibid.

7. The CERT Coordination Center (CERT/CC) addresses risks at the software and system level. CERT/CC focuses on identifying and addressing existing and potential threats, notifying system administrators and other technical personnel of these threats and coordinating with vendors and incident response teams worldwide to address the threats. It is part of Carnegie Mellon.

Chapter 5

Fraud investigation: Understanding the problem

Introduction

The phone rings . . . a surprise internal audit review has identified missing assets, or perhaps your company's routine fraud analysis has detected some unusual transactions. Fraud investigators are familiar with such a 'Friday afternoon call'. A discovery is made on the Monday, but a few precious days are lost as people in different parts of the organisation prevaricate and procrastinate before escalating it to the next level. Eventually, the decision is made to call in help at the end of the week – the delay is a function of uncertainty about what to do and shock that fraud could be happening so close to home.

Kenneth Farrow, the former Head of the City of London Police's Economic Crime Unit, describes the organisational paralysis that can follow the discovery of a potential fraud: "There is a period of disbelief. Somebody low down the pecking order thinks that something does not look right, but that individual is frightened to speak out initially and does two or three checks before they tell the supervisor. The supervisor does the same thing, because he doesn't want to look a fool by barking up the wrong tree. It's like a taxi meter; from the moment of discovery to the moment of reaction, the journey gets more expensive because you are losing ground all the time. The message to organisations is, 'If you spot it, go for it straight away, encourage your staff to speak out. Put it under the microscope at the earliest opportunity and let's begin an investigation.'"

In short, detection of a potential fraud is only the first part of the process; the organisation's response, especially in the critical early stages, will determine how it emerges from the crisis – whether it suffers minimal damage and gains some valuable lessons learned or, in exceptional cases, experiences total collapse of a division or the entire organisation.

The investigation itself is all about gathering, processing and analysing information to arrive at evidence. Evidence is a legal concept and the strict legal definition in relevant jurisdiction will be practical to an investigation that ends up in formal legal proceedings. Any situation you choose to investigate will be awash with information – evidence is information that passes two tests: that of being reliable and that of being relevant.

In this chapter we discuss some of the aspects of initiating, controlling and closing out an investigation and avoiding the potential pitfalls, such as missing the big issues by getting sidetracked by minor issues, or trampling over evidence and mishandling witnesses and suspects such that the investigation process itself exacerbates the damage to the organisation.

Defining objectives

The purpose of investigating is usually to understand what has happened, take appropriate actions and move on, armed with lessons and insights that can help the organisation in the future. This sounds like a simple aim, but often other organisational objectives affect how an investigation is handled and actions are prioritised. Some common objectives are described in the following table:

If we want to . . .	Think about . . .
Recover stolen funds or other assets or make an insurance claim	What type of evidence will the courts or insurers expect?
Take disciplinary action against employees	What are the relevant HR or employment law considerations for how we deal with these individuals?
Provide assurance to the stakeholders – employees, investors, regulators and other interested parties	How will we communicate the strategy, progress and outcome of the investigation?

The relative importance of these and other factors to the organisation means that the overriding objective, and therefore strategy for each investigation, is unique. While one company may just want to get the stolen money back, in some sectors such as pharmaceuticals or financial services, reputation is everything. In such organisations, the concern will be more centred on what the incident portrays about their culture and how their employees are incentivised so that they can make the necessary changes.

Robert Hunter, a Partner at Herbert Smith Freehills specialising in the recovery of stolen assets, explains: "Very often, the least of all the problems is that the fraudster wants to keep the money and the company wants it back. The company may be more concerned to know how it happened and what technique was used. This will enable it to avoid a reoccurrence of the fraud."

Do we need to investigate?

Not every report or suspicion merits an investigation. Generally, very specific allegations, either from credible sources or, in the case of anonymous reports, those incorporating details which can be verified through an investigation, pass the 'assessment' test. In other cases, the organisation should revert to the source and seek specific information in relation to the allegations. The case of the Madoff whistleblower, Harry Markopolos, is an example of how detailed and reasoned allegations *should* ring alarm bells – his report to the regulatory authorities incorporated a financial model to support his case that Madoff's numbers were literally too good to be true: a monthly return on investment of 1–2% every month, 96% of the time, with no volatility.

In practice, it is rare for an allegation to be reported with an accompanying evidence dossier, but vague allegations will need to be clarified to enable the company to investigate. For example, those manning whistleblowing hotlines should be trained to obtain detailed information regarding the precise nature of the allegations, including names, dates and amounts.

When do you change direction or decide to stop?

The Oil-for-Food programme, which we mentioned in Chapter 2, was a $60bn initiative to enable the Iraqi government to buy food and humanitarian supplies with the proceeds of oil sales. The programme was riddled with corruption and there followed multiple investigations, continuing over many months, to uncover what had happened.

Similarly, major corporate collapses such as those of Enron and WorldCom, triggered major, complex and lengthy investigations. While most investigations are at a much smaller scale, they all have one thing in common – their investigation requires the development of well thought through 'fraud hypotheses' which can be tested by reference to the available facts. In scientific research, the objective of a hypothesis is to provide a plausible explanation that can be tested. A fraud hypothesis is just that – a logical explanation of how a fraud could have been committed and the nature of the evidence trail it would have left.

Care must be taken not to jump to conclusions and any quick explanation should be treated with some caution. It is natural for those within an organisation to try to justify the first explanation for an incident of apparent fraud or a set of unusual transactions. This is often achieved through explaining away any contradictory factors that undermine the initial assessment. The challenge is that people are not always aware that they are doing this. Instead, they believe that they are making perfectly rational judgements. In fact, they are accentuating the evidence that fits their predetermined ideas.

A more appropriate approach to the investigation involves starting with the hypothesis - which is one possible explanation for what has happened. This will help to guide the investigation so that this hypothesis is tested against the available evidence. Where evidence is identified that disproves the hypothesis, then an alternative explanation needs to be defined and tested using the same approach. In this way, the fraud investigator behaves like a research scientist - testing the hypothesis and searching for inconsistencies until none remain.

The fraud hypothesis is a product of professional judgement of the investigators in the light of the allegation and available information. Based on the results of the investigation as it progresses, the hypothesis may need to be refined. The investigation must remain focused on prevailing hypotheses. This approach will lead to a logical path to closure, where the 'story' of the fraud can ultimately be told. This approach is illustrated in the following train of thought:

- It was suspected that . . .

- Our hypothesis on how this could have happened was . . .

- Then when we looked at the evidence and saw that it supported/contradicted our hypothesis . . .

- And so, based on the evidence, we conclude what happened was . . .

- And here's what we should do now . . .

A fraud response process that you can stand by

A serious incident of fraud is often preceded by a series of incomplete or inadequate investigations of less serious matters. A robust and transparent response, allied to comprehensive investigation process that can stand the test of scrutiny is essential.

Rather than create a detailed set of instructions on how such a response should look, we have highlighted some of the critical factors that need to be considered.

An important aspect relates to the way in which laws and regulations differ between jurisdictions. This brings a significant level of complexity to those who are conducting cross-border investigations for multinational organisations as, for instance, witnesses may have different rights depending on their nationality or physical location. The consequences of ignoring such differences can be significant and the success of an investigation can hinge on whether investigators have considered local laws. Each case will be different, but taking such matters into account throughout the planning and execution of an investigation will help to mitigate the risk of its failure.

Building the right team

Putting together a team with the right skills, experience and independence to investigate the situation is fundamental.

- The team needs to be sponsored at the appropriate senior level within the organisation.

- The core team will need to have access to other key personnel such as HR, internal audit, in-house counsel and compliance officers and experienced fraud investigators.

- In jurisdictions where there is a concept of "legal privilege", the choice of team will also be influenced by the decision on whether the investigation should operate under this legal protection.

- Steps to be taken to decide on the involvement of the police and/or regulators, and who should liaise with them.

How to deal with suspected employees

Whilst the finger may be pointing at one or more specific employees, they do of course remain innocent unless and until the allegation is proven. There are a number of principles that should be followed:

- Be fair.

- Ensure that the relevant management is fully aware of the company termination procedures and take legal advice on what action should be followed.

- Consider the need for consultation with works councils or other employee bodies.

- Confirm that the suspect has no physical access rights to buildings, clients or computer systems.

- Emphasise that the team should not allow the suspect to have unsupervised access to company records or computer equipment while suspicions are being investigated.

- Comply with relevant laws, rules and employment regulations.

Interviewing witnesses and suspects

A key source of information will be the suspected individuals and witnesses. Full advantage of each and every conversation needs to be taken and there are rules which must be followed to protect the rights of all parties:

- Ensure that the requirements of the disciplinary and legal process have been adhered to through seeking appropriate legal advice.

- Interviews should be held by a senior member of staff with a designated note-taker.

- Detailed notes should be taken of all conversations and meetings held with the suspects.

Collecting and handling evidence

Evidence is fragile and securing it can be fundamental to the success of the investigation. The team must therefore:

- Collect all related original documents from the premises and from external sources.

- Record where/from whom the document was collected.

- Ensure compliance with relevant privacy and data protection legislation, taking legal advice if necessary.

- Ensure that the original documents are copied and protected from damage.

- Limit the number of times the original documents are handled, as they may be needed for evidence purposes.

Dealing with electronic information

The collection and preservation of electronic material in particular presents a number of challenges. The first challenge is to maintain its integrity and provenance. There are well used and established procedures to assure the authenticity, reliability and traceability of such data – procedures which will survive legal challenge.

In addition, data privacy requirements vary from jurisdiction to jurisdiction and care must be taken to ensure that such regulations are not breached.

- Identify all computer and other electronic/digital assets that the suspect has access to, and where possible secure these assets and limit further access. This will include:

  - Obtaining details of all the suspect's current access rights.

  - Freezing the suspect's IT network and remote access until the investigation has reached a conclusion.

  - Restricting the suspect's access to landline, mobile phone or other telephone accounts registered to the company.

- Secure computers used by the suspect.

  - If the computer is in a powered-down state, do not power it up but remove all leads and cables.

  - If the computer is switched on, do not access the computer by any means (locally or remotely), as important and vital information may be lost. In this instance, call for immediate specialist computer forensic assistance.

  - Ensure that all computer evidence is forensically imaged and secured.

  - Ensure that the suspect's e-mail accounts are forensically secured.

  - Ensure that any networked storage areas used by the suspect are forensically secured.

- Ensure that the relevant file server(s) and other back-up tapes are removed from the back-up cycle and secured. This may be crucial to tracking events over a period.

- Secure system, Internet and other relevant log files and audit trails where available. These logs can provide evidence of the suspect's activities over time.

- Contact an independent specialist for help.

Communicating with staff

One of the harmful effects of a fraud (whether it is an allegation that is ultimately proven or one that is not), is the damage that may be done to staff morale. This means that effectively managing the communications is important:

- Keep as much information as possible confidential. In the early days of an investigation, it is often not possible to identify all those who will be implicated.

- Ensure that a consistent message is communicated to staff and other stakeholders.

- Remind staff of their confidentiality obligations to prevent details being leaked to outside parties.

Communicating with the media and other interested parties

Despite the countermeasures, a significant incident of fraud is likely to result in rumours that are likely to spread outside of the organisation. Proactive steps need to be taken to manage the media and other stakeholders such as regulators, customers, suppliers and insurers:

- Inform the designated press officer of the suspected fraud at the earliest opportunity.

- Agree a statement that can be used when necessary.

- Ensure that all calls received by employees are routed to the press officer.

The aftermath of the fraud investigation

The impact of a fraud is likely to extend beyond the boundaries of the organisation and it is important to consider when and how to communicate with such stakeholders which could include customers who need to be compensated for losses. The company itself may be able to recoup losses if appropriate insurance cover is in place.

The discovery and subsequent investigation of a fraud is likely to be a very draining experience, testing morale and company resilience. Loyalties and commitment will also be put under pressure as staff members are interviewed, raising suspicions where none need exist and causing unnecessary doubts and perhaps a lack of confidence. To that extent, it puts the onus on the HR department to handle the innocent parties, leaving the lawyers to deal with the criminal perpetrators.

The message therefore for management is both to isolate the incident, and make an assessment on whether also to keep looking forward beyond the immediate problem depending on whether it is an isolated occurrence or just one of many related issues. They need to send a message that the issue is being dealt with, that it is temporary and that the damage suffered is reparable. The organisation will be far stronger for having dealt with it properly.

Learning the lessons

A fraud, particularly a large one, will teach an organisation a great deal about itself. It may, for example, learn that it needs to alter its overall attitude to fraud and fraud risk. Other outcomes may include:

- Systems and controls may have failed to prevent the fraud – these will need to be fixed and employees trained to be more vigilant.

- Detection mechanisms may have been too slow to react to the early warning signs or may have failed to pick them up at all.

- The ethical tone of the organisation may be found to be at fault, whether through causing the fraud to take place or through allowing it to happen.

Experiencing a fraud is the corporate equivalent of a personal trauma. Although traumatic experiences are damaging, they can also make individuals more resilient in the long run. The same is true of an organisation – emerging from a major fraud incident with robust anti-fraud defences and a change in a management style which rewards ethical behaviour.

What next?

If a significant value of assets has been stolen, then the focus of the organisation can move to the next phase – asset tracing, often a long and complex exercise. In the words of one commentator, "Asset recovery is a slog. It requires hacking through thickets of international law."[1]

---

1. "Making a hash of finding the cash", *The Economist*, May 2013

Chapter 6

Asset tracing:
Recovering the money

Introduction

Identifying and recovering assets following a fraud can be a frustrating and time-consuming process, as the shrewd fraudster will have made the movement of funds a complicated trail to follow. Just ask the creditors of Bernard Madoff and Allen Stanford, whose networks of companies and bank accounts, and rapid movement of funds across multiple jurisdictions, have taken investigators years to unpick.

To identify and recover assets successfully requires skilled, considered investigation, as well as a high level of understanding of company law, accountancy, financial statements and corporate structures. For a sophisticated asset-tracing exercise, it is therefore important to have a team of lawyers on hand to navigate through the legal systems in the countries where the assets are located.

Any victim of fraud will understandably seek redress by recovering as much of the misappropriated wealth as possible, but the uninitiated will quickly find that there are many complexities in achieving that end, and success will ultimately depend on tactical thinking, perseverance and a little good fortune. Asset tracing is much like peeling away the wrapping in pass the parcel – the removal of each layer of deceit brings the investigator closer to the ultimate prize.

The role of the authorities

It can come as a surprise to a victim of fraud that their involvement in the investigation process does not necessarily diminish once they have reported it to the authorities. There is an expectation from the enforcement bodies, that where a company has been the victim of a fraud, it should undertake and fund its own investigation. Police forces often lack the resources or experience to investigate complex fraud cases and choose to focus on other categories of crime.

Embarking on a tracing exercise can be daunting for company management, who may not have been in such a position before. The sheer level of analysis and associated support required to meet the high standards of proof needed in criminal cases means this can be an expensive process with an uncertain outcome.

On receipt of a report from the company, the powers available to enforcement bodies are varied and include criminal proceedings, civil remedies, confiscation orders, restraint orders and asset forfeiture. Each of these requires input from courts and, as a result, cases can take years to come to conclusion. In the UK for example, a complex fraud case can take five years to reach the courts through a mixture of investigation time and legal process.

There are a number of advantages to the victim of fraud in pursuing criminal action. Enforcement bodies have wide-ranging powers to search and seize documents and property. They can detain suspects and, in certain circumstances, compel suspects and witnesses to answer questions. Government agencies and enforcement bodies often have information-sharing agreements at a national and international level – with overseas proceedings recognised by treaty in countries as diverse as Germany, India and Japan. These allow for expedited access to, for example, bank records from overseas accounts by issuing a letter of request. These powers may reveal information or assets that would not otherwise be identified.

But, even if there is a criminal conviction, funds may not be returned to the victim of the fraud. Countries vary significantly in their approach, and it is not uncommon for the state to issue confiscation or recovery proceedings following a conviction, but either to retain the recovered funds or fail to make any recoveries at all. This means that a victim of fraud may go through the entire legal process with little or no recovery of assets.

Civil remedies

The purpose of a civil action is to get financial redress rather than a criminal conviction, and the standard of proof required is usually lower as a result. Criminal convictions require a standard of evidence 'beyond all reasonable doubt', whereas in most countries a civil action requires a case to be established on the 'balance of probabilities' only. The facts of the civil case are considered by a judge who is experienced and knowledgeable about financial issues and well placed to consider the intricacies of a complex fraud scheme, which may escape the lay juror.

The combination of high cost, length of time and uncertain outcome has led victims of fraud to choose to pursue civil recovery. In general, this means an action brought by an entity or individual independently of prosecuting bodies.

There are a number of attractions to the victim of the fraud in pursuing the civil route. The process is likely to be fairly straightforward – filing a claim form with the relevant court with a 'skeleton' case outlining the basis for the claim or complaint and the evidence that supports it. That case will be built around a 'cause of action' under that country's law – either for fraud, misrepresentation or a similar provision. Each country will have its own framework for a complaint to be heard. The US civil procedure rules are a comprehensive example, providing clear guidance to be adhered to by both parties as the case progresses.

There are many remedies available to the courts prior to the claim proceeding to trial at which stage the case will need to be more thoroughly supported. The lower standard of proof in civil proceedings means that the level of analysis of evidence and the corresponding time and cost of the investigation can be reduced. Depending on the evidence and accompanying requests put forward by the claimant, these may include orders that freeze the assets of the defendant, require the defendant to disclose the level and location of their assets, compel respondents to provide the claimant with copies of relevant documentation or compel the defendant to surrender their passport.

Powerful remedies such as these can quickly progress an investigation whilst giving comfort to the victim that there are identified funds available for recovery if the case can be successfully established. The claimant retains control of the investigation in a way that is not possible in a criminal case, and it is likely that the case will reach trial within a far shorter time due to the reduced level of complexity of evidence. The defendant may even agree to settle prior to the case going to trial, saving time and expense for both parties.

As with criminal prosecutions, there are disadvantages to the victim of the fraud in pursuing a civil action. The costs of the investigation and action are initially borne by the claimant and, in the event that the action is not successful, it is likely that there will be an order made for the claimant to meet the costs of the defendant. In addition, pursuing a civil action alone will not lead to a conviction and associated punishment, which does not always sit comfortably with a victim of a fraud.

Civil and criminal actions are not necessarily mutually exclusive, and there can be benefits to their being launched in parallel if there is information sharing between the parties. But the path may not be smooth; the involvement of enforcement bodies may mean that witnesses are reluctant to cooperate with a civil investigation, and the fraudster may claim that the civil case prejudices the criminal proceedings, leading to a stay of the civil case pending the conclusion of criminal proceedings.

Risk versus reward

The decision about whether to opt for criminal or civil action should be considered in the early stages of an investigation, as it will determine the scope and approach of the investigation team. Ultimately, the decision is rarely clear-cut due to the differing circumstances of each case, but the primary driver for the majority of corporate clients in proceeding with either course of action is simply 'will we get any money back?'

The thought of the management time and effort required is often at the top of mind for companies. Uncertainty about the outcome and the potential cost is usually the first concern, swiftly followed by the justifiable questioning of whether there is in fact a commercial upside from either option, if successful.

There is no precise science to weighing up risk versus reward, but a staged, commercially focused approach gives the greatest chance of recovery. Such an approach should assess the costs of action, the likelihood of success and, importantly, the pool of assets available from which to obtain recompense.

Understanding the financial interests of the target of a potential claim is therefore vital, and clearly the value of the asset pool should significantly outweigh the likely costs of pursuit. Targeting an individual who has no assets makes little sense. An assessment of the potential prize enables the victim of the fraud to take an informed view on whether it is likely to be commercially beneficial to launch or continue civil action, whether criminal action is the best route or whether to simply write off the losses as a lesson learned.

The initial asset assessment

The complexity of the initial asset assessment will vary depending on the case. The director of an owner-managed business who defrauds a lender may have previously provided the bank with a personal guarantee, with a supporting list of assets. This is clearly a more straightforward verification exercise than is likely when dealing with a long-term, predatory fraudster, who has deliberately siphoned off many millions from a company and made every effort to put his assets out of reach.

That said, the basic approach will remain the same: methodical reviews of available information, the application of a heavy dose of cynicism and an effort to put yourself in the shoes of the subject of your investigation. What do we mean by this? Well, consider a fraudster who regularly holidays in the same area of the world. Is it a huge leap of faith to think that he may own a property there? The flamboyant fraudster with the jet-set lifestyle – could he own a plane, boat or helicopter?

These hunches may well lead nowhere, but enough imaginative think-ing at the outset can give you leads to assets you may not otherwise have identified.

The investigation team will have access to a variety of information sources as they undertake the assessment, ranging from company records, bank statements, corporate filings and asset registers to indi-rect sources, such as Internet blogs and media stories. Gathering and filtering this information is vital in building a picture of the assets which may be available for pursuit and their likely location.

In the early days of any initial asset assessment, anecdotal evidence can be of significant importance. Fraudsters are not necessarily discreet, and it is very likely that individuals working alongside them will hold vital back-ground information. Very early into a recent case, a witness who was the subject of the investigation had repeatedly discussed a sizeable home he was building on the coast. In another, the fraudster had emailed pictures of his classic car collection, complete with registration numbers, to a colleague.

Communications with third parties will need to be carefully managed to avoid accusations of slander, but, in the case of an employee fraud, it is reasonable for the victim of the fraud to ask suppliers or customers to provide details of stock movements or payments if there are concerns about their legitimacy. In another recent investigation, a simple letter to a number of suppliers identified that rebates due to the company for bulk purchases had been paid by cheque at the request of a certain employee. They had never been recognised in the books of the victim and, instead, had been cashed by a business established with a very similar name that was controlled by the suspect.

Online information can vary in age and accuracy, but Internet search engines can throw up valuable details of assets from court filings, credit reporting, property websites and planning applications. There is a diverse range of information available. An investigator seeking aircraft in Australia, residential properties in Portugal or container ships in Saudi Arabia will find registers to help with each of these tasks. The biggest fraudsters often have some form of public profile, and press stories routinely contain references to assets – even boastful quotes from the fraudsters themselves. The mix of personal indiscretion and gossip prevalent in social media adds an additional, and sometimes entertaining, dimension to this, but careful interrogation can flag up relationships or backgrounds that provide further leads for investigation.

A recent development to aid this process is software that undertakes systematic searching of websites, asset and corporate registers in multiple jurisdictions and languages. For example, access to translated media stories originally written in Russian or Urdu, or information taken from South American corporate registries, provides intelligence that would previously have proved difficult or impossible to obtain without a huge investment in person hours.

Access to company records, including email and bank statements, may yield other evidence of assets controlled by the fraudster. It's not uncommon to see email communications relating to the purchase of properties or vehicles, containing insurance schedules listing antiques, or conversations that flag up transactions requiring further examination. Analysis of accounting transactions can identify unusual supplier or customer relationships, round sum transfers to bank accounts controlled by the fraudster or payments for assets that the company has never been in receipt of.

The value of corporate information

The fraudster may well be a director or shareholder of various corporate entities, with some of their interests more obvious than others. Corporate structures can be used to shield assets, and it is therefore important to consider and map them fully in order to identify whether there are other asset-bearing entities connected to the subject of your investigation.

Corporate filings can tell you the value of the company, the particulars of its major assets and who its directors and shareholders are. Where a corporate entity or entities themselves hold the position of shareholder or director in a company, continuing to follow this trail to the end, through the next tier of corporate filings, can lead you to other entities owned or controlled by the subject of the investigation – or, potentially, by close friends or relations.

Where financial statements are filed, these may well disclose transactions with related parties, providing an additional set of companies and individuals to scrutinise. United States Securities and Exchange Commission filings in particular require a significant level of disclosure and may expose links to offshore entities that would otherwise not be apparent.

Clearly, the usefulness of corporate filings does vary. Publicly accessible registers exist in many jurisdictions but, whilst countries like the UK, Germany, India and (generally) the US, for example, require a high level of disclosure, this is not the case in other jurisdictions. In Jersey, for example, beyond the annual returns filed by the company – which do not have to include details of directors, shareholders or assets if it is not a public company – there is little other information available without formal country level cooperation or a court order.

In the British Virgin Islands (BVI), there is no easily accessible register of company names – let alone a list of company directors and their various directorships akin to that available in the UK. For a fee, it is possible to request confirmation as to whether a company is registered in the BVI and to request copies of filed documents, but there is no requirement for a company to file accounts, and the information the company has to disclose in filings is very limited.

Corporate information can therefore be opaque and gaining access to useful records may be difficult, but, in an environment of increasing regulation, this may be changing. An example of this relates to the issue of offshore trusts, which, in many locations, are the ultimate shareholders of a company or group of companies. This has historically frustrated the investigation process, as trusts often operate under a cloak of secrecy (in the Cayman Islands, for example, there is no formal register of trusts and there is no method of determining who is the beneficiary of a trust). However, increasingly stringent money laundering legislation has exerted enormous pressure upon the trust industry and resulted in a move towards increased transparency.

Even in jurisdictions where filing requirements are limited, looking back at historic records can identify directors, shareholders or financial information not present on more recently registered documents. So, whilst it would be misleading to suggest that it is always possible to lift the corporate veil, by being systematic and persistent it is often possible to gather significant levels of information on ownership and corporate value to inform the initial asset assessment and to be considered as part of the wider recovery strategy.

Decision time

The output from the initial asset assessment should be a schedule setting out a preliminary assessment of identified assets, value and jurisdiction. Registers of vehicles, property and shares exist in many locations, but there are also comprehensive international registers and databases with details of the ownership and whereabouts of boats, planes and many other categories of asset. These are valuable tools in testing ownership of the assets identified to date.

At this stage, a decision needs to be taken as to whether continued action is merited. The decision will be based on a combination of factors, including the estimated value of the assets and the costs and difficulties in taking control of them. Whilst there are occasions where companies will instruct their legal team to take recovery action regardless of the costs, in order to send a message to the marketplace or to punish the individual, those instances are increasingly rare. It's usually a straightforward commercial decision.

With this in mind, the investigation teams should work closely with the legal team to provide all relevant information to inform the appropriate legal strategy, which should be based on:

• The status of the assets to be recovered – including the asset's liquidity, ease of recoverability, whether it is likely to be declining or appreciating in value and other parties who may have claims over the same assets.

• Where and how to mount a claim – the findings from the initial investigations may lead to parallel actions in one or more jurisdictions. Jurisdictions will differ in levels of co-operation and transparency, which will impact on the speed and likelihood of success in recovery of assets.

• The impact of civil versus criminal claims, as already discussed – for example, in certain jurisdictions it is possible to freeze, but it may not be possible to penetrate banking rules' secrecy for a civil claim.

- Applicable tracing principles – these are internationally recognised and can be applied to follow misappropriated funds and to distinguish them from 'clean' funds with which they may have been mixed. Determining those principles that will lead to the greatest recovery is often complex, yet critical to maximising recoveries. Complications can arise where assets have been sold to a purchaser acting in good faith or where bank accounts that are the destination of stolen money contain a mixture of criminal and innocent funds. It will ultimately be for the court to decide on ownership and what remedy to apply.

The recovery strategy

Where a decision to pursue civil action is taken, various options are available to the victim of the fraud. Expert legal guidance is necessary in order to ensure the option selected is proportionate to perceived risk.

There are a number of options which will incur little in the way of cost:

- Continuing with the claim until it reaches its conclusion, without taking any action to protect or preserve the asset pool, may well be the right course of action when dealing with a simple fraud – theft by an employee, for example – where the investigation team are satisfied that there are few liquid assets and therefore dissipation is not a risk.

- Where assets have been identified, gaining and enforcing a summary judgment (agreement from the court that the defendant has no real prospect of successfully defending the issue) on a straightforward element of a claim can give the victim of the fraud confidence that there will at least be some return and these may then be used as a 'fighting fund' to take further action in relation to larger heads of claim.

- Working towards an agreed commercial settlement may well be the best solution, reducing the cost burden of a prolonged court case.

There are also many tools available to assist in the protection and identification of assets where there are concerns around dissipation, or where further information is needed to identify assets and trace movements of funds. The measures set out below are those frequently used under the English common law system, but similar provisions exist or are recognised in many jurisdictions, and many of the key offshore centres, such as the Channel Islands, Cayman Islands and BVI, default to the English common law position.

Freezing order

A freezing order is granted by the court over assets owned, or believed to be owned, by the suspected fraudster up to a value commensurate with the estimated quantum of the fraud. It can be granted across a body of assets, specific assets or, on rare occasions, may be unlimited in scope.

An application for a freezing order is invariably made on an ex parte basis (i.e. without prior knowledge of the defendant) and will set out the grounds for the application. The claim does not yet need to be fully articulated, but it should be sufficiently detailed for the judge to conclude that there is a solid prima facie case to answer by the suspected fraudster, that assets are at risk unless they are frozen and that information may be lost or destroyed unless it is seized.

The victim of the fraud must make full disclosure of all known facts, even those which do not assist his case. He will be required to confirm that he would be liable for appropriate damages in relation to the order, should it later transpire it should not have been made. It is important that the application is well drafted, and the significant input required from the investigation and legal teams means that gaining a freezing order can therefore be an expensive process.

A freezing order is a draconian measure, and the court will not grant one unless convinced that there is a risk that the defendant will abscond or that the assets will be dissipated. Robert Hunter, a leading specialist lawyer in this area, says: "Where the person in question is an international jetsetter and there is a strong prima facie case of dishonesty against him, you can go to the court and get an injunction against him outlining the assets and asking for those assets to be frozen. Very often, the court will require the fraudster to deliver up his passport."[1]

The freezing order is therefore a very powerful tool. Once granted, it can be served on any institution known or believed to hold assets owned by the fraudster and on the fraudster himself – advising that the assets to which the order relates cannot be dealt with or disposed of. The court may grant an order requiring various institutions to deliver up documents under request, such as bank statements, which can then be reviewed for evidence of transfers to other accounts or for the purchase of assets. This may provide additional evidence that others are involved in the fraud and open up another avenue of claim to pursue.

The order will either be specific to the country in which it is granted or international in scope (a 'worldwide' order). Such an order is not automatically recognised overseas, but individual institutions may elect to observe it as a matter of policy. Many jurisdictions will observe an order from an overseas jurisdiction once it has been registered in their local court – in a case where there are assets in multiple jurisdictions, lining up hearings to take place in each locality in quick succession is optimal, though can be logistically challenging.

Not only does the order require that the fraudster ceases to deal with or dispose of his assets, he is also required to provide full disclosure of the location, details and value of all the assets he owns or holds up to the value of the claim (failure to do so can lead to imprisonment). This is a huge advantage to the investigation team. The fraudster may disclose assets that have not yet been identified, but may also fail to disclose assets that *have* been identified, putting him in breach of the order and providing evidence to the judge that he is untrustworthy, which is unlikely to be in his favour when the fraud claim reaches trial.

Robert Hunter says that a freezing order is, "hugely attractive in tracking down fraudsters . . . you have got the person and once you have him, you have his knowledge and his documents, and that gives you the insight. Once you have a prima facie case of fraud . . . a freezing injunction, it gets much easier to seize the assets. People tend to pay money from one account to another. Sometimes I get people saying they don't have bank accounts, but usually, they say they have one; then you can see what has been paid in and paid out or transferred."

In exceptional circumstances, the court may grant a 'search' order which allows the applicant to enter premises accompanied by a supervising solicitor in order to search them for documents or electronic records relevant to the case. This is rare and would require a very strong prima facie case that there was incriminating material on the premises which was at the risk of destruction.

The Norwich Pharmacal order

Sophisticated fraudsters will channel misappropriated funds through as many bank accounts as possible, in order to complicate the trail and make recovery more problematic. Often, funds move many times between accounts held by numerous companies in a multitude of jurisdictions.

The bank, lawyer or accountant holding the funds at the point of the investigation will nevertheless, be under a duty to their client, even if they themselves are completely innocent of any involvement in the fraud, limiting their ability to provide information to the victim of the fraud or their advisers about the provenance of the monies held.

This presents a problem for those seeking to trace these funds. The UK House of Lords' decision in the case of Norwich Pharmacal provides a way of dealing with such conflicting duties. This decision established that the following must be established in order for the court to grant an order:

- The respondent must have been involved in some form of wrongdoing – in some way, facilitating it.

- The information requested is necessary to assist the victim of the fraud in attempting to seek redress.

The Norwich Pharmacal order is a very valuable tool to enable the process of asset tracing. If it can be demonstrated that stolen funds have been moved to an account in another location, this order can be used to mandate the receiving bank to disclose information about the account, its owners and the subsequent movement of the funds. This will lead the investigator to other accounts in relation to which further orders can be obtained. In this way, the funds are followed from account to account, and from jurisdiction to jurisdiction.

The next step has a number of hazards, warns the lawyer. "When the Norwich Pharmacal order enables the client to find that the money has gone to a particular jurisdiction, he may be tempted to get an order in that jurisdiction freezing the money. That is all well and good if the money is there, but a freezing injunction puts the other side on notice. As soon as you get the injunction, you have to serve it. Then you have notified them of your interest and the game is up. If the money has gone from there, you have frozen an empty account."

Insolvency as a tracing weapon

The insolvency practitioner is in a privileged position when it comes to undertaking an asset-tracing exercise. Whilst they vary by jurisdiction, an insolvency officeholder's powers often include the capacity to compel individuals and entities to provide documentation or submit for interview, if that would assist the officeholder in recovering money for the estate.

These powers of compulsion are hugely beneficial in gaining access to documents and data that would otherwise be out of reach and can be used to investigate significant leads. There is well-established protocol for the recognition of overseas insolvency powers in local courts, a considerable help in cross-border cases.

Taking insolvency proceedings against the fraudster, or entities owned by him, may therefore be another option to aid the recovery exercise. Compulsory powers may then be available in order to gain access to the next tier of financial information and, potentially, assets, which can be a vital tool in an asset-tracing exercise.

An example of this is a case where a network of companies registered in seven jurisdictions was controlled by a single individual. Over a period of several years, a financial institution provided lending to one of those companies (Company A), unaware that its management was effectively operating a Ponzi scheme.

Company A fell behind in its repayments to the bank and, as a result, was placed into liquidation. It was evident to the liquidator from examination of Company A's bank statements that the borrowed funds were not used legitimately, but instead transferred to the other companies' accounts. The liquidator was then able to use compulsory powers to compel the recipient bank to provide details of where that money had been transferred.

In a case such as this, where there is no legitimacy to the transactions that have taken place, there are provisions in insolvency legislation for them to be voided or set aside by the court. The transfers of funds could be considered to be 'transactions defrauding creditors' or 'transactions at undervalue' and therefore repayable to Company A by the recipient companies.

When, as is likely, repayment does not take place, the liquidator can take recovery action against the recipients, and those entities can themselves be placed into liquidation. This provides access to the books and records of this next tier of companies (including, potentially, email traffic which may assist in evidencing the fraud), control of any assets and visibility of historic fund movements. This tracing process can continue until the ultimate destination of the funds is reached.

Liquidators can exercise these powers to compel anyone they believe has relevant information to cooperate with them. Unlike a Norwich Pharmacal order, there is no requirement for liquidators to make application to court to use the power of compulsion; it is theirs to use as they see fit. That is not to say that they will not require the assistance of the court if the bank does not submit; failure to co-operate with a liquidator in this manner can be punishable by fine, imprisonment or both.

Conclusion

The hunt for assets is never going to be easy. An asset assessment is an iterative process, with each new piece of information potentially needing the investigator to revisit earlier conclusions as links between individuals and entities become apparent. Each step will provide the investigative team with a host of leads to follow, each of which will need to be tested in the search for assets.

In this chapter, we have set out a selection of the options and tools available to the victim of fraud when seeking to recover funds. When considering the elements required to undertake a successful asset-recovery exercise, they can be boiled down to just three aspects: the right team, the right tactics and the right approach – and that little dose of good fortune!

Key considerations for the victim of fraud seeking redress

1. Take professional advice at an early stage – asset tracing can be daunting, and experienced lawyers and forensic accountants can help you navigate through some of the minefields.

2. At the outset, consider your desired course of action – civil, criminal or both – and structure your activities accordingly.

3. By focusing on identifying potential assets, you can adopt a staged commercial approach that is flexible, tailored to the circumstances of the case and proportional to the outcome.

Dishonest directors

Administrators were appointed over a European wholesale distributor by the company's bankers. The company had traded profitably for a number of years, building a network of suppliers and manufacturers in Asia, but had latterly begun to experience cash-flow difficulties as a result of a market downturn.

The administrators based themselves at the company premises as efforts were made to sell the business. During that process, concerns emerged that the directors had caused stock to be moved out of the business for nominal amounts in the run up to the administration, thereby reducing the level of assets available for creditors.

A number of company employees were interviewed to gain understanding of the events leading up to administration and to probe the concerns already identified. A combination of these interviews and a review of historic company emails revealed that the directors had also been causing the company to overpay amounts to suppliers before diverting the 'repayments' from suppliers into offshore accounts in their personal names.

The investigation team began to identify other issues, such as personal expenditure for vehicles and antiques being disguised by the creation of false invoices, and the sale of stock to connected parties at a significant undervalue. Within two days of arriving on the premises, they had identified that nearly £2m had been drawn out of the company by its directors in a variety of schemes – effectively funded by the bank.

The investigation team set about establishing what assets were still held by the directors by reviewing email traffic, interviewing employees and undertaking searches of publicly available information. They uncovered a portfolio of properties, antiques, and classic cars, funded by monies improperly drawn from the company.

With the bankers facing a substantial loss on their lending, a decision to undertake a more comprehensive investigation was taken, and the administrators reconstructed the historic trading of the company by reviewing electronic accounting material and piecing together a comprehensive evidential picture of how the various schemes had been perpetrated. Armed with an affidavit outlining these findings, and concerned about the risk of flight, they gained an ex parte worldwide freezing order over the various assets and offshore bank accounts identified by the investigation.

The freezing order was served on the directors at one of their overseas properties and on banks in the US, the UK, Portugal and Ireland. Requests for full bank statements swiftly followed, and a comprehensive review of them led to further requests for copies of cheques and electronic transfer documents in the search for other assets.

A full claim was prepared and issued by the administrators, and various defences submitted by the directors were discredited following further investigative work. A meeting was arranged where a settlement was negotiated, leading to a significant recovery for the benefit of creditors in the administration.

The directors' conduct was reported to the appropriate enforcement bodies, in order that disqualification proceedings could be commenced against them.

Barlow Clowes – an early model for asset tracing, freezing and retrieval[2]

The process of tracing, freezing and recovering the proceeds of a fraud perpetrated by Peter Clowes and his fund management company Barlow Clowes is regarded as a model for receivers and liquidators of fraudulent assets to this day. In fact, the story goes back to 1988, when regulators and police launched an investigation which was the first of its kind in the then newly deregulated UK market.

The discovery that Clowes was paying investors – mostly retired nurses and teachers – out of the contributions from new investors was made by regulators already suspicious of the above-market interest rates he was offering on UK government securities. More than 14,000 investors in the scheme faced losing their money – an estimated £170m in total.

Two strands of investigation and process were launched. On the criminal side, police (and subsequently the Serious Fraud Office) were brought in to examine what was then one of the largest known Ponzi schemes in the UK. Their investigation resulted in a criminal trial in 1992, at which Clowes was convicted and sentenced to 10 years in prison.

On the civil side, the regulators brought in receivers (and joint liquidators in Gibraltar) to seek to regain the fraudulently acquired assets. A law firm was appointed to trace, freeze and recover assets. Clowes had spent considerable sums on a notoriously lavish lifestyle, owning a private jet, a large yacht and country houses.

A civil claim was started in the civil courts against the primary defendant, Peter Clowes. An order was obtained, asserting that he had breached fiduciary duties in respect of a sum of money, a freezing order was granted and a disclosure order was issued against the bank to which funds had been transferred.

Records produced under the order showed the trail taken by the stolen funds, and this led to other banks which were similarly required to disclose the whereabouts or movement of funds. Each time funds were traced, they were frozen. The same applied to Clowes' possessions bought with stolen funds which could then be recovered by the receivers.

It should be noted that the process works only in common law jurisdictions, such as the BVI and Gibraltar (a key Clowes base), but not in civil law jurisdictions, where the same concepts and remedies may not be available.

In parallel with the pursuit of assets directly stolen from investors, receivers had another set of targets from which to recoup lost funds. These were companies which cooperated with the fraudster, and could or should have known that Clowes was behaving illegally. The receivers were able to make claims against them on the basis that they benefited from the fraud directly or indirectly.

Companies that received funds were identified and a demand issued for the return of the funds. If the funds were not then returned, then this may be used as a basis for putting the company into provisional liquidation. This would give the receivers access to the company's records so that they could understand where the assets are located. The most high profile of these cases was Barlow International vs Clowes Eurotrust International. The latter was an Isle of Man company whose owner, Peter Henwood, was found by UK judge Lord Hoffmann to be 'liable' in respect of claims from the Barlow Clowes company that was in liquidation.

The receivership was successful, with some 90% of the lost money recovered. In fact, the investors were already out of the picture by this stage, as the government had made good 90% of their losses, following a high-profile lobbying campaign focused on the fact that the government (criticised for maladministration by the Parliamentary Commissioner for Administration) had failed to regulate the Barlow Clowes funds. Best says the government recovered £156.5m out of £170m lost, although the funds were only handed over to the British government in February 2011 following an order by the Supreme Court of Gibraltar.

1. Interview with Robert Hunter, Herbert Smith Freehills

2. Interview with Roger Best, Clifford Chance

Chapter 7

Corporate irresponsibility?

Introduction

Can an entire organisation become so riddled with fraud and corruption that it, in itself – as opposed to the individuals working for it – is treated as a perpetrator of fraud?

In this chapter, we consider how we have reached a point where prosecutors are treating organisations as a 'single fraudster' – with organisational fines, prosecution of board members and the imposition of expensive and ongoing remediation and monitoring programmes – and the implications that this has for individual board members.

"When a director of a major company plays even a small part [in a fraud], he can expect to receive a custodial sentence." This was part of the judge's summing up as he sentenced three directors of the 150-year-old UK bridge-building firm, Mabey & Johnson, for paying bribes to Iraqi officials as we described in Chapter 2. The company pleaded guilty to corruption. More recently, in the UK, the scandals in relation to the misselling of payment protection insurance (PPI) and interest rate-hedging products (more commonly referred to as 'swaps') have battered the already-tarnished reputation of the banking industry. In the case of PPI, UK banks have set aside huge sums to be used to compensate consumers to whom the products were inappropriately sold. By mid-2013, media reports were estimating that costs would be up to £18bn – a sum that also includes the costs associated with reviewing and processing the claims. As with previous breaches of corporate compliance, such as serious deficiencies in anti-money-laundering systems, this is a clear illustration of how corporates bear the costs of the investigation, the required remediation and ongoing monitoring activities demanded by the authorities.

A more cross-industry problem, the allegations of misconduct amongst the banks that set key interest rates – initially in relation to the London Interbank Offered Rate (LIBOR) and subsequently to other, similar indices, such as those for Europe and Singapore (Euribor and SIBOR) – has drawn the attention of regulators, prosecutors and class-action lawyers from around the globe. Initial costs, fines and settlements have been significant, although in fact relatively small in comparison with those relating to the PPI issue. Perhaps the highest profile case was seen in mid-2012, when it was revealed that one of the banks involved, had been fined a total of £290m by the UK's Financial Services Authority (FSA), the US Department of Justice and the US Commodity Futures Trading Commission (CFTC) – in itself, a clear example of increasing cross-border regulatory coordination.

A further significant development in relation to the LIBOR case is that it has since been referred to the UK's Serious Fraud Office (SFO), which has the task of determining whether there is sufficient evidence that there is a criminal case to answer. Quite apart from any criminal liability that is found – whether in relation to the corporate bodies themselves or their directors – it is anticipated by some analysts that the costs of litigation and damages may eventually dwarf even those of the PPI issue[1].

Regulatory trends

The current regulatory direction is summarised by Jonathan Cotton, a Partner at Slaughter and May: "There is going to be a much greater compliance burden placed on corporates and their boards. A company will be liable for misbehaviour, such as bribery, unless it can show it took steps to avoid that kind of conduct." This is a specific comment about the UK Bribery Act, but it reflects a much more widespread trend that started many years ago in the US.

Deferred Prosecution Agreements

Deferred Prosecution Agreements (DPAs) and the related Non-Prosecution Agreements (NPAs) have been commonly used by the DOJ in the US in relation to breaches of legislation, including those relating to violations of the Foreign Corrupt Practices Act (FCPA). In such circumstances, the agency agrees to either defer prosecution or not to prosecute the company. In return, the company pays fines and disgorges the profits arising from the improper activity. In addition, it agrees to reform relevant processes and procedures and cooperate fully with subsequent investigations. A process of monitoring may also need to be put in place to ensure compliance with the terms of the agreement. Historically, companies have employed third-party 'monitors' approved by the regulator, but there is an emerging trend of companies being authorised to self-monitor through their compliance and internal audit functions.

In the case of DPAs, once the terms have been satisfied, including those that define the period of on-going monitoring, the prosecution of the company will be discontinued and no further proceedings taken. In contrast, NPAs do not contain conditions relating to monitoring and satisfactory performance, although they retain the elements of financial penalties, disclosure and cooperation.

The principle behind these agreements is to provide some limitation to the level of damage to a business as a result of corporate criminal proceedings. Otherwise, the impact of the prosecution and unintended consequences may extend to corporate collapse with devastating impact on employees, customers, suppliers and other third parties.

The DPA is now a tool that is at the disposal of UK prosecutors under Schedule 17 of the Crime and Courts Act 2013. David Green QC, Director of the UK SFO, placed the bar high, when he outlined the conditions that needed to be established for the granting of a DPA: "DPAs are aimed at corporations, not individuals, and generally speaking, they are aimed at historic misbehaviours. If the same board that condoned misbehaviour is still in place, there is no way they will get a DPA. Not everyone will get a DPA and not everyone will be offered a DPA, only in pretty tightly controlled circumstances. The company will need to pay for an investigation and reach a sensible settlement."

Criminal negligence

DPAs should also be seen in the context of developments, such as the introduction of the UK Bribery Act. This includes the principle that a company will commit an offence if, after being found to be engaged in bribery, it fails to demonstrate that it followed adequate procedures to prevent bribery. This is only the latest in a series of initiatives, including those relating to money laundering and the proceeds of crime, which have successively put greater burdens on organisations to put in place appropriate systems and processes to control the activity of employees and their other representatives.

Self-reporting

Companies that anticipate becoming the subject of a fraud or bribery investigation by an external agency have a number of options. The first step will, of course, be to undertake an internal enquiry. This should be consistent with the highest standards and involve expert investigators. In Chapter 5, we discussed aspects of an investigation in more detail.

The company will then need to assess the gravity of the facts. In the first instance, if it has not already done so, management will need to inform both the audit committee and the external auditors. Where the firm is subject to specific local requirements, such as for those who are part of the UK's 'regulated sector', and the fraud is sufficiently substantial, the firm will make a statutory report to the appropriate authority. The company may also elect to report the suspicion to other bodies including law enforcement agencies, and regulators. Often the company will be subject to the jurisdiction or supervisions of a number of regulatory bodies. In some cases, the best strategy will be to make simultaneous disclosures to all of relevant parties.

If it decides to make such a report, the nature of the relationship between the corporate and the authority needs to be established. The assistance of competent legal and business experts, familiar not only with the company's rights under the prevailing law, but also with the enforcement agency's practices, personnel and latest thinking, will be essential.

When the company takes this route, it is making the clear statement that it is being open and transparent. However, there may also be a defensive and tactical purpose, as a proactive disclosure may help to suppress the suspicion that it is seeking to hide something. Conversely, "the company that harbours such information but does not disclose it exposes itself to reputational risk", says Louise Delahunty, a Partner at the law firm Sullivan & Cromwell. "You need to look very carefully at whether you need to bring this issue to the attention of the government, so that the company is perceived to have done the right thing. If the company doesn't and then is found out, its reputation could be badly damaged."

The company that makes the report must be prepared for the response of the agency. Where the agency wants to take the case further, it may want to work with the company, gaining the benefit of its investigatory resources, its documentation and its witness material.

In the UK, for instance, the fact that an organisation has reported itself will be a relevant consideration to the extent set out in the Guidance on corporate prosecutions[2]. This guide explains that, for a self-report to be taken into consideration as a public interest factor tending against prosecution, it must form part of a "genuinely proactive approach adopted by the corporate management team when the offending is brought to their notice".

While organisations continue to regard the self-reporting route as a helpful way to deal with information they may hold about a suspected fraud, its value as a means to building a positive relationship with the law enforcement agency appears to have been dimmed by some statements issued by David Green QC. Set against this is the fact that the SFO faces severe budgetary restraints, constraining its scope to mount high-level investigations.

The case for self-reporting – cartels

Nowhere are the benefits of the self-reporting of inappropriate behaviours demonstrated more starkly than in anti-trust cases. The 'race for leniency', as it is commonly known, involves members of a cartel seeking to be the first to disclose details of their involvement in collusive, anti-competitive activity. The rewards for being the first to blow the whistle are significant. Fines in such cases are typically calculated as a percentage of the affected sales – in large markets, this can represent hundreds of millions of Euros – and those that are first to cooperate benefit from significant discounts.

The European Commission's approach was explained in 2006.[3] The first firm to provide evidence of a previously unknown cartel may receive total immunity from fines. Other cartel members who voluntarily provide additional, value added evidence may expect subsequent fines to be discounted according to a sliding scale – the suggested discount for the first such firm is between 30% and 50%, the next between 20% and 30%. Remaining cartel members who provide valuable information may expect fines to be discounted by 20%.

The Dodd–Frank Act on Conflict Minerals

A further illustration of the tide of change is shown by certain elements of the US Dodd–Frank Wall Street Reform and Consumer Protection Act[4] and the provisions under Section 1502 in respect of 'conflict minerals' emanating from mining operations in the Democratic Republic of Congo and nine adjoining countries. Under the terms of this legislation, which applies to SEC 'issuers', companies are required to make disclosures in relation to their usage of such minerals.

The underlying effect of these requirements is that companies need to assess their supply chains proactively, conduct appropriate due diligence and, potentially, publish a Conflicts Minerals Report. The company is required to conduct due diligence using a nationally or internationally recognised framework such as the OECD Due Diligence Guidance for Responsible Supply Chains of Minerals from Conflict-Affected and High-Risk Areas[5]:

1. Establish strong management systems.

2. Identify and assess risk in the supply chain.

3. Design and implement a strategy to respond to identified risks.

4. Carry out independent third-party audit of smelters'/refiners' due diligence practices.

5. Report annually on supply chain due diligence.

The legislation is still new and companies are gaining an understanding of exactly what is expected of them. Similarly, there has been no indication or experience of what sanctions might be levied on those that fail to comply with the requirements. It is clear, however, to those covered by the Dodd–Frank Act that compliance will be a significant and expensive effort.

Components of the response

So, the demands on organisations to deal with fraud and corruption are increasing. Such organisations can start to put themselves in a better position to deal with these demands through a focus on three main areas:

Systems

Organisations must seek to ensure their policies and the associated controls meet the leading practices of compliance and ethics. Guidance in such standards may be obtained from a range of sources including, for instance, the OCEG[6] and the Committee of Sponsoring Organizations of the Treadway Commission (COSO)[7]. This means that, if a suspicion arises, there is a greater chance that it can be quickly addressed.

Relationships

Maintaining good relationships with the relevant regulators and law enforcement agencies can be a useful proactive strategy for almost any organisation. In addition to ensuring that lines of communication are open in situations where there is a need to make a disclosure, it may also provide a channel for intelligence on current and emerging risks in the industry. Achieving this can be a challenge as the regulatory landscape in many countries is often in flux as illustrated in the UK by the reallocation of the responsibilities of the Financial Services Authority to the Prudential Regulation Authority and the Financial Conduct Authorities.

Public relations

Once an organisation proactively manages fraud risk and its relationships with the authorities, it is in a better position to mitigate the reputational risks associated with the publicity of an incident. This may be achieved through the careful consideration of external communications with the media, shareholders and customers to present an account of the relevant facts, to correct erroneous information and to effectively convey the company's point of view. And, where things have gone wrong, acknowledge and follow up with decisive actions. The golden rule: make an admission, show contrition and fulfil your pledge to do better.

---

1. http://www.huffingtonpost.com/2012/08/27/libor-scandal-bank-cost-estimates_n_1833150.html

2. http://www.sfo.gov.uk/about-us/our-policies-and-publications/guidance-on-corporate-prosecutions.aspx

3. "Immunity from the reduction of fines: Leniency in cartel cases" Official Journal C 298, 8.12.2006

4. http://www.sec.gov/about/laws/wallstreetreform-cpa.pdf

5. See Annex 1 of OECD *Due Diligence Guidance for Responsible Supply Chains of Minerals from Conflict-Affected and High-Risk Areas* http://www.oecd.org/daf/inv/mne/GuidanceEdition2.pdf

6. http://www.oceg.org

7. http://www.coso.org

Chapter 8

Regional perspectives: India, Africa, China and the Middle East

Introduction

Lack of transparency, accountability and opportunity for personal gain fosters an environment in which fraud and corruption thrives. In many rapid-growth economies, institutions (such as a functioning civil service or independent judiciary) are in their infancy. This creates an informal economy along with unofficial processes for 'getting things done', which can increase the risk of fraud and corruption. This risk manifests itself differently in each region and, in this chapter, we focus on India, Africa, China and the Middle East.

Balanced against these increased risks, the potential rewards are high, as these markets have significant and growing populations of potential customers and workforce and in many cases natural resources. In addition, governments and other institutions in these markets are now taking steps to make them more attractive to investors and trading partners.

India

India has been recognised for some time as one of the engines of global growth, with a population that broke through the one billion barrier in the late 1990s and has continued to grow at a rapid pace relative to more mature markets. Allied to this growth in population, India's GDP almost doubled in the five years to 2010. India now stands as the 10th largest economy[1], with GDP at a similar level to Canada, Italy and Russia. By 2030, it is expected to be third behind only China and the US. As such, India is a very attractive market for investors and entrepreneurs and, unsurprisingly, this also makes it an attractive target for fraudsters. In recent years, the increasing focus on the success of the Indian economy has been matched by a growing awareness of fraud, bribery and corruption cases in the country. Widespread coverage of the extraordinary fraud at Satyam Computer Services and the massive 2G corruption scandal has highlighted to an international audience the risk of fraud and corruption in India.

But the rate of economic growth is not always consistent, and is periodically punctuated by times of slower progress. Such a period is now being seen in India where a series of less positive economic indicators have resulted in a reduction in confidence in the Indian growth story. Experience from other markets shows that periods of economic slow-down can heighten the fraud risks as individuals and companies come under pressure to satisfy market expectation of continued growth. It is also in such times that pre-existing frauds are often exposed – as Warren Buffet famously wrote in a letter to investors in 2001, "After all, you only find out who is swimming naked when the tide goes out."[2]

The Satyam story

Satyam was, for a long time, an example of Indian success, feted around the world as a market-leading business. Having started in 1987, the business, led by the Raju brothers, reported growth that helped to make it one of India's largest companies. This growth was further demonstrated when, in 2001, Satyam's shares were listed on the New York Stock Exchange.

This success story came to an abrupt end when, in January 2009, Ramalinga Raju publicly admitted to manipulating the reported financial performance of Satyam by systematically overstating revenues, assets and even its number of employees. Subsequent investigations by the Serious Fraud Investigation Office (SFIO) and the Central Bureau of Investigation (CBI) found that revenues at Satyam had been overstated by a total of more than $840m, supported by a complex system of forged invoices, forged bank statements and manipulated account-ing entries. The perpetrators also fabricated board resolutions in order to obtain $260m of bank loans and acquire land and property with a value of $74m through shell companies. Raju resigned from the board and was arrested. He was charged with criminal conspiracy, breach of trust and forgery, among other offences.

Satyam is a further dramatic example of the perils of believing a growth story that, in retrospect, was just too good to be true. The case is nota-ble for its similarities to other cases of extraordinary fraud that have been uncovered elsewhere in the world.

- The CEO was a dominant personality who faced insufficient chal-lenge from the board.

- The reported operating margins were significantly higher than indus-try norms.

- The CEO was personally involved in the preparation of the financial statements.

- The reported financing profile of the business was inconsistent – Satyam drew down significant loans from banks but also reported having large sums held in deposits.

The manipulation of results started on a small scale but grew out of control and obscured an underlying business that was in fact suffi-ciently sound such that it survived the crisis and was subsequently sold to a large Indian conglomerate. In his resignation letter to the board of directors, which was simultaneously released to the public, Raju said, "What started as a marginal gap between the actual operating profit and the one reflected in the books of accounts continued to grow over the years . . . It was like riding a tiger, not knowing how to get off with-out being eaten[3]."

This case illustrates an interesting theme; it shows that the character-istics of the fraudster do not necessarily change with geographic location; their behaviours simply adapt to reflect local conditions. In India, one important local characteristic is that family businesses account for a very high proportion of the country's private sector – 60% of the market value of its top 500 firms, a proportion that continues to increase[4]. Satyam was one such family business. It became a global business, but its leadership, management and governance arrangements did not keep pace with that growth, instead retaining structures based on family connections, with a small group of dominant decision-makers and little independent challenge. The Satyam story, and the economic significance of similar family-run companies, highlights interesting challenges for the future development of corporate governance in India.

2G licence scandal

Another recent example concerns the auction of 2G mobile telephone licences by the Indian government. On 24 September 2007, the Department of Telecommunications announced that the deadline for submission of 2G licence bids would be 1 October 2007. Later, in January 2008, having rejected or ignored interventions by the Prime Minister, the Ministry of Finance and the Ministry of Law and Justice, the Department of Telecommunications announced that contracts would be allocated on a first-come first-served basis to bids that had been received by 25 September 2007, thus denying later bidders the opportunity to acquire the licences. Following the allocation, several of the winning bidders re-sold their licences to other operators and, in the process, realised huge profits.

When, in 2012, it published its findings on the tender process, the Supreme Court of India described the auction as "illegal" and "wholly arbitrary, capricious and contrary to public interest . . . " The court immediately and unilaterally cancelled all 122 licences that had been awarded[5]. An investigation into the auction by the Comptroller and Auditor General (CAG) also confirmed that the auction process was severely flawed. The CAG determined that the failures in the auction process had deprived the Indian exchequer of approximately $34bn[6]. Mr Raja, the Minister of Telecommunications at the time of the auction, resigned from his position in 2010 and, in 2012, he was arrested on charges of corruption.

The case illustrates some interesting dilemmas for investors; a precedent had been set where businesses had their licences revoked despite claiming to have followed the process as defined and communicated by the Ministry. In such an environment, with its moving goal posts and common requirements for partnering with specified local companies, foreign investors can struggle to make long-term business decisions.

These and other incidents have fuelled a perception that there are high levels of fraud, bribery and corruption in India. For example, Transparency International's *Corruption Perceptions Index* ranked India 94th out of 176 countries in 2012[7]. Results from EY's 2013 EMEIA Fraud Survey[8] further support this view. Almost two-thirds of Indian respondents said that they were aware of revenue or cost misstatement at their company in the last year, compared with 20% of respondents from all nations. Furthermore, 69% of Indian respondents perceived bribery and corruption as widespread in this market, and a third were prepared to make cash payments to win business.

A legislative response

In 2011, growing public frustration at corruption in India sparked widespread protests, including those inspired by the anti-corruption campaigner Anna Hazare, and captured worldwide media attention. Supported by legislation such as the Right to Information Act (RTI) and Public Interest Litigation (PIL), campaigners have increasingly been given the tools to draw the focus on to financial abuse in the country.

The response of the Indian government has been unambiguous. A number of measures aimed at addressing corporate governance issues and the risk of fraud, bribery and corruption in the country have since been adopted. The Companies Act 2013, enacted on 29 August 2013, after the President's assent, will replace the 56-year-old Companies Act once it is fully notified by the Government of India. This Act enhances the powers of the SFIO and further defines board and senior management liability in the event of fraud. The Bill will also introduce the concept of class-action suits, giving investors a right to claim damages or compensation for any fraudulent, unlawful or wrongful act by companies in which they hold shares.

Other measures include The Prevention of Bribery of Foreign Public Officials Bill (2011), The Anti-Corruption Grievance Redressal and The Whistleblower's Protection Bill (2010), the ratification of the United

Nations Convention against Corruption (UNCAC) (2012) and the proposed Jan Lokpal Bill, which aims to create stricter regulations to control bribery and corruption. The 2012 Public Procurement Bill seeks to regulate and ensure transparency in the procurement process. This raft of new legislation could provide much needed impetus to changes in the corporate governance environment in India.

For example, companies will now be specifically required to adopt proactive measures as a result of proposed legislation, with a corresponding increased expectation that may help drive key changes in corporate governance. For example, Clause 177 of the Companies Bill requires every listed company to establish a whistleblowing mechanism (termed 'vigilance') for directors and employees. Industry bodies are also imposing more rigorous standards; for example, a fraud monitoring framework set up by the Insurance Regulatory and Development Authority (IRDA) sets out a requirement for businesses to take proactive measures, such as conducting fraud vulnerability assessments, third-party due diligence and training and monitoring of employees and agents.

While these proactive steps appear familiar, because they reflect best practice elsewhere in the world, there are also some fraud risk areas in India that require particular focus.

Financial services

According to figures published by the Reserve Bank of India, fraud losses incurred by banks increased by 88% from INR20bn between 2009/2010 and 2010/2011 and doubled over four years, exceeding INR38bn (approximately $680m). The CBI's Bank and Securities department registered criminal cases worth INR40bn (approximately $700m) in 2011. This scale of losses coincides with growth in the value of non-performing assets on bank balance sheets.

One of the schemes used to defraud banks is loan fraud. Arpinder Singh, FIDS leader for EY in India explains that, "Companies taking loans from a consortium of banks sometimes use fake documents. These practices are partially responsible for today's high level of non-performing loans." One company owner employed a middle man to bribe bankers in order to procure loans based on falsified documentation. A number of banks each provided loans secured against the same collateral, making recovery impossible. Whilst the loans went into default within a year, instead of being classified as fraudulent they were treated as non-performing assets. Rather than highlighting the extent of the fraud, the situation appeared to be one of poor lending decisions. The risk of such a fraud is much greater where a central register of mortgages and charges is not maintained.

In a recent high-profile example of loan fraud, eight top-ranking officials of public sector financial institutions and unnamed real estate developers were arrested by the CBI on charges of bribery and collusion after they bypassed bank due diligence procedures[9]. In a separate case, a number of public sector banks were accused of receiving illicit payments from real estate developers to sanction large-scale corporate loans. These actions overrode mandatory conditions for such approvals. Borrowers have also been found to mortgage the same property to a number of different banks to raise funds when the lender fails to conduct appropriate due diligence.

A common theme in these cases is that of fraudsters taking advantage of weaknesses in information systems – where information is not monitored or shared, or data is managed locally and not consolidated, it is easier for institutions to be misled. Management guidelines issued by the Reserve Bank of India now require bank staff in treasury and key relationship management roles to rotate their positions and to take mandatory periods of leave. Private and foreign banks are advised to appoint 'chief internal vigilance officers' to oversee compliance. In parallel, the CBI is developing a Bank Case Information System (BCIS) to act as a repository for information on known bank fraudsters. Field officers in the banking sector will have access to the database[10].

A changing social landscape

In a country with a relatively young population, it should come as no surprise that this is also reflected in the age profile of fraudsters. Arpinder Singh says, "Fraudsters are changing. In the old days, the fraudster was often a middle-aged person or someone in senior middle management who could make a decision. Now, younger people are engaging in fraud." This is not to say that the risks of the past have gone away; indeed, recent research found that, while senior management were only involved in 23% of cases overall, they were involved in 79% of 'major' fraud cases (defined as those cases involving over INR100m, approximately $2m). However, there is a growing risk that, as technological and social changes increase the access younger employees have to commercially sensitive information, their ability to significantly impact the organisation will also increase. Some recent examples of novel fraud schemes illustrate the way in which changes in Indian society are being realised:

• Fraudsters posing as representatives of well-known multinational companies charged potential recruits a fee to be placed with the company. This type of advance fee fraud is particularly common in the IT sector, where competition for jobs is intense. Senior investigators commented, "They took the money from desperate job seekers and disappeared. It is the number one fraud, especially in the high-tech industry where so many people are being hired." In addition to the losses incurred by the legitimate candidates, these frauds harm the reputation of the business that is being impersonated.

• Counterfeiters have access to branded goods through scrap packaging, inadequate disposal of obsolete stock or theft of finished goods. Accordingly, counterfeit products can be assembled with minimal investment: a significant risk for high volume products that require low-assembly effort. Counterfeiting leads to loss of revenue, erosion of customer satisfaction, damage to brand integrity, price distortions and the development of a grey market for these goods.

• Incidents of stolen data and fraud have raised concerns about privacy and data protection in India. This is exacerbated by the threat posed by cyberfraudsters and others who misuse technology. In one case, a group of software engineers whose requests for higher wages had been denied, used computer viruses and malware to cripple the air traffic control system that they had constructed at an airport. This action resulted in major disruption and the airport's temporary closure.

Doing business in India

Although India continues to be a favoured destination for foreign investment, growth opportunities are constrained by regulation and bureaucracy. The World Bank ranked India 132nd out of 183 economies for ease of doing business, 181st on dealing with construction permits and 182nd for enforcing contracts. The World Economic Forum *Global Competitiveness Report* ranked India 96th of 142 economies for burden of government regulation.

For example, in the construction sector, builders have reported requirements to obtain numerous licences, from multiple government bodies in order to construct a property. In one case, a builder was required to obtain 57 approvals from 40 departments of central and state governments and municipal corporations, and provide 170 documents to obtain the licences[11].

The combination of a market with significant investment potential and a high level of bureaucracy has resulted in some organisations seeking to bypass, accelerate or influence decisions, including engaging directly or indirectly in acts of bribery and corruption. Ongoing education of employees and agents on the rules and regulations, and their personal responsibilities for compliance, is an important measure for managing this risk.

Africa

Over the past decade, many parts of Africa have seen reforms in macroeconomic management, improved incentives to encourage private sector activity and increased demand from the international markets for the natural resources with which many African countries are richly endowed. As a result, African GDP has more than tripled over this time[12] and, according to *The Economist*, GDP grew faster in Africa than in East Asia in eight out of the 10 years from 2000[13]. Yet perceptions of Africa as an investment destination have not shown concomitant improvement. Although there has been a recent upturn in attitudes, some African countries still struggle with a prevailing view that governance is weak and controls for managing the risks of fraud and corruption are inadequate.

Although estimating that foreign direct investment projects would amount to $150bn by 2015, EY's *2012 Africa Attractiveness Survey* of more than 500 investors and business leaders highlighted the 'stubborn perception gap' that continues to hamper efforts to attract investment into the continent: "Africa is still viewed as a relatively unattractive investment destination compared to most other geographical regions." The report also noted that high-profile enforcement actions by Western regulators for corrupt conduct in Africa play a part in this negative perception. The extreme income differentials that exist across most of the region also pose a major challenge, and present a barrier to addressing bribery and corruption. According to Charles de Chermont, FIDS leader for EY in Africa, "It is difficult to solve these problems and perceptions when you have islands of wealth in a sea of poverty."

Measurement of fraud in Africa

A number of recent studies have consistently reported high levels of fraud, bribery and corruption in Africa. For example, EY's *12th Global Fraud Survey* found that respondents in Africa (by comparison with responses to the same questions in other geographies) were "most likely to have experienced a significant fraud in the last two years". However, when attempting to understand these figures in more detail, it is important to recognise the diversity of conditions and cultures that exist across the continent and acknowledge that local circumstances vary considerably.

Furthermore, fraud, bribery and corruption levels in Africa are likely to be inconsistently reported and, in some places, understated by published figures with a substantial range in the quality of reported information impeding attempts to make comparisons between countries. For example, the reporting of cases is influenced by the differences that exist between countries in terms of the reputation and record-keeping of institutions such as the police and judiciary, as well as being fundamentally linked to local attitudes in relation to what should and should not be reported.

EY's *Europe, Middle East, India and Africa Fraud Survey 2013* (the 2013 EY EMEIA Fraud Survey) highlights some of the differences in the nature of the threat faced by organisations in different parts of the continent.

The survey drew responses from Kenya, Nigeria and South Africa. Whilst pressure on results was a consistent theme across these three nations (with more than three-quarters of those surveyed in each country agreeing that there was "increased pressure to deliver good financial performance"), it was clear that corruption was seen as a greater threat in Kenya and Nigeria where 94% and 89% indicated that "bribery / corruption practices" were widespread.

Nigeria was perceived to be a place where companies most commonly overstate their financial performance (with 68% agreeing compared with 35% for South Africa). However, South Africa was seen as a place where foreign businesses were regulated more closely – although the differences were not quite so stark.[14]

Legal developments

Considering the level of attention paid to fraud, bribery and corruption, observers are often surprised to learn that many African countries have signed up to the OECD Anti-Corruption Convention and already have robust legislation in place to address these risks. Some countries' laws give power for extra-territorial reach and many legal codes ban 'facilitation payments'. A facilitation payment is made to a government official, such as a customs officer, to induce them to change the way in which they perform a routine function, rather than to affect whether that function is performed at all. In that sense, a facilitation payment is distinguished, for the purposes of the Foreign Corrupt Practices Act (FCPA), from a bribe.

Tackling corruption is also the goal of the African Development Bank Group's recently launched Anti-Corruption and Fraud Investigation service. Furthermore, in recent years, African regulators have started to bring derivative actions against companies already under investigation by US prosecutors for alleged FCPA violations.

Doubts remain over the rigour and consistency with which incidents of fraud, bribery and corruption are identified, investigated and prosecuted. Some commentators point to the relatively low salaries of local officials and judges, which make these officials more vulnerable to corruption, whilst political intervention also remains a very visible problem. Such challenges were highlighted by Patrick Lumumba, the former head of the Kenya Anti-Corruption Commission (KACC). On his removal in 2011, amidst allegations of political and judicial interference, he commented, "In my view, those who engage in corruption are now emboldened because they believe that they can always deal firmly and effectively with those who dare to fight corruption without any consequences."

Significant risk areas

Taking a step back from this, a picture of significant real and perceived fraud risk is emerging which interacts with potentially inconsistent and corruptible authorities. But to what should organisations pay the most attention? Experience helps us to identify a few of the key risk areas.

Tendering and contract fraud

Bringing sufficient accountability and transparency to the procurement process remains a significant challenge, with many cases of collusion between customers, suppliers and competitors. Insufficient or ineffective oversight of key budgets has led to controls in both public and private sector organisations being repeatedly defeated. Charles de Chermont points out that, "Collusion is easy to do and difficult to pick up, as benefits agreed between supplier and procurer may be paid in kind, such as employees having their holidays paid for or their children's school fees settled."

The relationships between civil servants, politicians and businesses facilitate collusion, especially as the disclosure of interests is often inadequate and sometimes well below the standard required by law. The public and private sectors both play a role: much is said about public sector corruption and bribe-takers but there is also a bribe-player on the other side of the transaction. Regular movement of employees from public to private sector roles, encouraged by the higher salaries on offer, helps to maintain these networks. Some of the more common tender and contract fraud schemes that we have observed include:

• Submitting separate, apparently independent bids from companies that are actually under common control in order to achieve the minimum number of tenders required by the rules.

- Manipulation of tender specifications to favour a particular supplier.

- Issuing revisions, new information or timetable amendments in a way which favours a particular supplier.

- Sharing confidential and commercially sensitive information received from one party with their rival suppliers.

- Signing separate contracts with the same supplier in different locations.

- Members of the contracting team holding an interest in one of the suppliers.

To counteract this, organisations that are involved in a tendering process must remain vigilant for any sign of this kind of activity and even withdraw from the process where the facts indicate that the tender has been fundamentally compromised.

International aid

With governments in mature markets still struggling to balance budgets and reduce deficits, aid programmes are coming under increasing scrutiny. Agencies are now expected to demonstrate that aid is being used effectively and appropriate steps are being taken to reduce the risk of fraud, bribery and corruption.

Organisations distributing some of the $50bn in aid and financial support that Africa receives every year have been targeted by fraudsters[15]. In addition to the large-scale procurement scams described above, recent examples include the following cases:

- A gang operating in Kenya and Tanzania manufactured invoices for hotels and travel costs. They sold these to local employees of a non-governmental organisation (NGO) to support fraudulent expense claims. The documents were relatively sophisticated, being tailored to each claimant's circumstances.

- In a separate case, another NGO neglected a large plot of land in Kenya that it had acquired as part of a development project to house animals. Fraudsters exploited this neglect by fabricating land sale documents and 'selling' the property to another party.

Offset obligations

There is ever more regulatory scrutiny of offset obligations following increasing concern that negotiation with government officials can be used as a covert way of paying bribes. Offset agreements are found most frequently in contracts in the defence, oil, gas or mining sectors. These typically involve the contractor committing to either fund or undertake additional activities, such as infrastructure development in the contracting country.

One reason for concern is that the details of these offset agreements are not always made public or negotiated in a transparent way. These agreements should be made as part of the tender process, with clear and formalised terms that can be enforced.

Taking advantage of ethnic quotas

Fraudsters are also exploiting quotas imposed by governments to encourage a fairer distribution of economic and social benefits. This is illustrated by the Black Economic Empowerment Act (BEE) adopted in South Africa in 2003, which mandates affirmative action by setting quotas for the ethnic composition of company shareholders or borrowers from an institution. Such mandatory requirements can open the door to abuse.

For example, a practice of 'fronting' has emerged where a market has developed in the use of the names of people qualifying within a quota category, sometimes without their knowledge. In other cases, junior employees have been officially recorded as shareholders in order to meet quotas. Businesses may also register individuals who are completely unconnected with the company as directors and name these people in official correspondence. On occasion, these individuals have deliberately agreed to 'front' so as to win contracts and then pass on the business to higher-charging firms.

Taking this a stage further, some companies are also thought to have deliberately underreported their revenues in order to increase their likelihood of winning tenders from a government that favours smaller, black-run organisations. Companies have used these tactics to 'improve their BEE scorecards', and so misrepresent their position when compared with competitor firms.

Fronting of this kind gives the false impression that the composition of business is changing more rapidly than is actually the case. In June 2011 the South African Department of Trade and Industry began consultations to make fronting an explicit criminal offence[16]. Controls to outlaw such practices include requiring identification documents to be checked prior to the signing of contracts. Stringent sanctions are now being discussed and a complaints procedure set up, linking fronting to a breach of the Companies Act, with an ombudsman appointed to monitor compliance.

Natural resources

Africa is richly blessed with natural resources – with huge oil reserves and extensive mineral wealth. With such riches there is a paradox – often known as the 'resource curse' – where the presence of such wealth has a harmful, rather than helpful, effect on the monetary wealth of nations[17]. This has been explained in terms of a number of factors, one of which is the increased levels of fraud and corruption that accompany the commercial exploitation of such resources. In light of the features that, as described previously, distinguish many African societies, this should not be surprising – adding wealth into a system that is unprepared for it is likely to create significant problems.

Nigeria, for example, is estimated to have lost $6.7bn between 2010 and 2012 as a result of the fraudulent activities of petroleum importers[18], who forged or counterfeited documents to qualify for state subsidies. The objective of the subsidies was to maintain petroleum product prices at affordable levels, but some importers fabricated bills of lading to exaggerate the extent of the imports, increasing the subsidy that they received. Others have claimed subsidies for product that has been imported into the country and immediately exported to another destination. The problem is reflected in the number of fuel importers to Nigeria, which leapt from five in 2006 to 140 in 2011, as fraudulent firms have been formed to exploit the scheme. By mid-2013, as a result of actions to reduce fraud losses, this had been reduced to just 30 accredited organisations.[19]

An initiative targeting this type of corruption is the Extractive Industry Transparency Initiative (EITI). Although the EITI has a global remit, the significance of natural resources in Africa means that many African countries are key members of the EITI. One of the main objectives of the EITI is to establish how much is paid for natural resources through annual public disclosure by companies and governments of the value of relevant payments. Such disclosure also enables the comparison of government and company information to help identify discrepancies.

The *EITI Progress Report* for 2013 highlighted that, in 2010, the Democratic Republic of Congo received just $876m in revenues from oil and minerals. This equated to just $13 per person – extraordinarily low for a country that, in the same year, produced half of the world's cobalt and a third of the world's diamonds.

In the same report, the EITI noted that, in Nigeria the transparency initiative had highlighted missing tax revenues for 2010 totalling $8.3bn, of which only $443m has been recovered.[20]

As a result of the EITI's efforts, transactions with governments have become more transparent. Local industry-led initiatives are also beginning to emerge in several African countries, composed of international companies operating in the region, local and international law enforcement agencies and local regulators. Databases where members provide details of companies with which they have experienced fraud, bribery or corruption issues are being established to act as references for members considering engaging with a new supplier.

China

As one of the largest and fastest-growing economies, China wields an ever greater influence over many African states as it seeks a secure supply of minerals and oil to feed the huge resource demands of its economy. We now consider the fraud and corruption risks and regulatory landscape in China itself.

Introduction

Recent media coverage of fraud and corruption in China confirms that it is a significant issue, but also suggests that there is an increasing willingness to engage with and tackle the problem. While in the past, according to Stephen Tsang, Professor of Contemporary Chinese Studies and Director of the China Policy Institute at the University of Nottingham, action against fraud was hindered by the widespread view in China that it was a victimless crime, "A time will come when it will change, but it takes recognition that there actually are victims to corruption, there are victims to fraud". That recognition is now taking shape in the form of new legislation and high profile convictions.

Political context

The political as well as regulatory community has corruption in its sights. Xi Jinping, the President of China, has made strong statements against corruption since coming to power in November 2012. Shortly after taking office, the President made a speech in which he made a commitment to pursuing corruption at all levels of society: "We must uphold the fighting of tigers and flies at the same time, resolutely investigating law-breaking cases of leading officials and also earnestly resolving the unhealthy tendencies and corruption problems which happen all around people."

There are two agencies at the forefront of the anti-corruption drive. The Internal Discipline Committee is concerned with official corruption by members of the Communist Party whilst the State Administration for Industry & Commerce (SAIC) is responsible for investigating corruption in the private sector. Further, in 2011, the Chinese Government passed the Eighth Amendment to the Criminal Law of the People's Republic of China. For the first time under Chinese law, this criminalised the payments of bribes to foreign government officials. This applies to all Chinese citizens, all persons located in China and all companies organised under Chinese law.

In parallel with legislative changes, there are moves to increase public access to information. In 2012 China's Supreme People's Procuratorate announced that provincial-level databases listing individuals and companies found guilty of bribery offences would be integrated into nationwide records. Once implemented and provided the information is publicly accessible, this would support the vetting of business partners by internal and foreign investors.

The impact of legislative and political changes is visible through increasingly high profile cases. Senior members of the ruling communist party who have been the subject to such action include Bo Xilai, a former member of the Politburo, and Liu Zhijun, who was the Railways Minister. These high profile investigations and prosecutions are reminiscent of the President's speech on investigating the "tigers" as well as the "flies" – targeting corruption amongst the elite as well as lower down the chain.

Other regulatory activity

Chinese regulators have also taken a tougher line on fraud across many sectors including financial services and pharmaceuticals. With a focus on China's capital markets, the China Securities Regulatory Commission (CSRC) has played an active role in the investigation and prosecution of fraudsters. Their plans, as announced by Xiao Gang, the head of the commission, include increases in the size of financial penalties along with moves to increase both the incentives offered to whistleblowers and the compensation paid to the victims of fraud[21].

The complexity and volume of cases which the CSRC and other Chinese law enforcement bodies are facing is growing rapidly. Reportedly, the number of cases grew by 21% year-on-year in 2012, and criminal cases were up 40% year-on-year in the first half of 2013. More than half of the cases involved insider trading, with a rapid increase in the incidence of fraud involving securities issues and information disclosure. According to the CSRC's 2012 annual report, fines and confiscations for the year amounted to a record RMB437m (just over €50m).

In some respects, the current momentum started back in 2007 when China initiated the move towards adopting international standards of accounting and started to make amendments to company law to address commingling of corporate assets by shareholders.[22] Commentators observed that this may have been a signal of the government's will to strengthen the judiciary's hand in combating corporate fraud.

Business relationships

Historically, business interactions in China have relied upon personal relationships rather than formal contracts. Chris Fordham, FIDS leader for EY in Asia–Pacific, observes that historically contractual documentation has often been quite vague and minimalistic. Deals could be concluded on a couple of pieces of paper and with a few signatures and "chops" - small stamps used to validate the document. Long-standing loyalties or family ties can often be more important in forming the basis of an agreement.

However, times are now changing. The country is in a transition towards a more formal structure of business. John Auerbach, an EY FIDS partner observes: "We are moving from a relationship-based system to something more contractually driven. The evolution towards a standardised, formalised way of doing business is a consequence of doing business on a larger scale. At some point, it is impossible to expand a business with only your friends and family, and there is a greater reliance on contractual arrangements with others." However, it can be hard for those unfamiliar with business practices in China to build trust and connections and also to distinguish between bona fide business relationships and those that may involve conflicts of interest, fraud, bribery or corruption.

For example, supply chain, collusion and conflicts of interest have long been live issues and areas to watch include:

- Authority: has significant authority been vested in an individual purchasing manager who is able to operate with minimal oversight?

- Distributors and other intermediaries: is there a third-party between the company and the customer or supplier and, if so, for what commercial purpose?

- Growth and controls: has the control structure kept pace with growth of the business? The controls put in place for 300 vendors are not the same controls needed where there are 3,000 of them.

Collusion between distributors and sales executives to inflate sales: "Channel stuffing"

This is a fraud scheme whereby distributors collude with sales executives by taking goods on to their books to inflate sales figures. The distributor is covered by a 'side guarantee' agreed with the salesman that addresses the risk that the latter is left with unsold goods. These goods are often passed from one distributor to another. Chris Fordham says that, "If the distributor is clever, he would have taken the goods on the basis that, if the deal falls over, there is a liability to take the product back. Where that is the case, the first company shouldn't be recognising the revenue right now, because it has not transferred the full risks and liabilities associated with that product. Unfortunately, the company finds that there are a set of previously undisclosed side agreements which leave them holding excess inventory. In the high-tech world for example, the inventory could quickly become obsolete, and the company is left to bear the losses."

Availability of information

A further challenge when seeking to conduct business in China is the insufficiency of background information on which to base an assessment of a potential partner's legitimacy. Performing such due diligence presents a particular difficulty as little information is publicly disclosed. Data about the ownership of companies and the background of directors is very limited and, where it does exist, it is sometimes outdated and maintained in hard-copy form only. John Auerbach says, "The documentation on vendors and customers is limited. It's hard in general to find out who owns the company, who the investors are and who manages it. The process is still fairly opaque. It's easy for the unscrupulous to take advantage of that lack of transparency, and filter purchasing dollars to themselves and their friends."

Moves, which started in Hong Kong, and now also being adopted in mainland China, have resulted in further restrictions to public information on companies and individuals. This action is in response to perceived external security threats, but could make managing fraud, bribery and corruption risks significantly more challenging, particularly in the context of the widespread use of nicknames and aliases. Companies seeking individuals' identity characteristics need the unique number from a Hong Kong identity card or the passport number in mainland China.

As a consequence of these factors, there is currently limited information in the public domain and research on individuals and companies is predominantly focussed on enquiries through networks of contacts.

Financial statement scandals

An interesting development over the past few years has been a wave of accounting scandals involving Chinese companies who had sought to access US capital markets. Between 2007 and 2010, more than 150 Chinese companies went public on US exchanges through either reverse mergers or initial public offerings.

However, against a background of accusations of impropriety and shareholder lawsuits, it has become clear that some of these companies have taken advantage of these listings to commit fraud. This is illustrated by the fact that by mid-2013, the SEC Cross-Border Working Group had brought 65 fraud cases against such companies and their executives.

The recent case of China MediaExpress, reported in 2013, illustrates the problem[23]. The SEC reported allegations of false reporting, which, according to the charges, started as soon as the company had successfully become a publicly traded company. As an example, the SEC cited circumstances where the company had falsely claimed within its 2009 financial statements to hold cash balances of $57m. In reality, the cash it held amounted to just $141,000.

In response to such cases, the US Public Company Accounting Oversight Board has been working with Chinese regulators to deal with the problem[24]. A Memorandum of Understanding between these two bodies, signed in 2013, is one example of the increased cross-border cooperation.

The context for the momentum of anti-corruption legislation and enforcement is China's position as a country that attracts massive foreign direct investment – over $70bn in the first seven months of 2013. The Chinese government has made, and continues to make, structural changes to maintain investor confidence and anti-corruption legislation and enforcement is part of that bigger picture.

The Middle East

The Middle East is a region that is best known for its huge resources of oil and gas. With the largest and most accessible reserves, many of the region's states are also amongst the richest in the world. This means that they also have significant influence across the globe through their investment interests that are typically made through sovereign wealth funds. But there are other countries which do not have the benefit of such reserves and so are dependent upon traditional economic drivers.

For example, the region is diverse in many respects, including political, religious and business environment. The current instability of Syria and Iraq contrasts with that of Saudi Arabia and the United Arab Emirates (UAE). This is reflected in the perceptions of corruption with the TI CPI ranking Syria (144th) and Iraq (166th) at the extreme end of the scale, with the UAE (27th) and Saudi Arabia (66th) at the other.

The findings of the 2013 EY EMEIA Fraud Survey tell an interesting story of the similarities and differences within the region, with 66% of respondents from Saudi Arabia saying that bribery and corruption were widespread in the country and that just under a third were prepared to offer gifts or make cash payments to win work. This contrasts with 6% saying they were prepared to misstate financial performance. Responses from those in UAE were noticeably different, with 24% saying that bribery and corruption are widespread in the country. Twenty-two percent said that they would offer gifts and 28% that they would be prepared to make cash payments. However, despite the region's differences, a common theme is the demographics. The young make up a very large proportion of the population, creating unique opportunities in the telecommunication, education and retail sectors. At the same time, the real and perceived geopolitical risks remain for business – including ensuring compliance with sanctions through due diligence on local partners and monitoring of fund flows.

Trust and culture

Culture and history influence business relationships everywhere, and the Middle East is no exception. The business culture in the Middle East places importance on personal relationships, some of which is built around the family. The level of trust given and expected in such relationships is a key part of doing business, which can blur the boundary between the personal and the professional. Bob Chandler, an EY FIDS partner explains, "In the context of a rational business decision, a manager may say it is better for me to use my brother's company to build this factory, because I can make sure I will get a good price and he does a good job."

The contrast between a rule-based and a relationship-based culture has been highlighted by others. Professor John Hooker, an academic at the Tepper School of Business at Carnegie Mellon University, commented, "Westerners organise their business around discrete deals that are drawn up as contracts or agreements and enforced by a legal system. Other cultures may organise their business around human relationships that are cemented by personal honour, filial duty, friendship or long-term mutual obligation."

Although relying on relationships and trust can have significant benefits for business, the apparent blurring of the boundary between family and work is sometimes difficult for organisations from other locations to deal with. It is accepted wisdom in Western organisations that conducting business with entities that are closely connected to their employees is undesirable and, therefore, employees should be discouraged from having such related interests. As a result, any potential conflict of interest that is disclosed is carefully managed. In contrast, according to Bob Chandler, "In the Middle East, it is common to have many business interests, rather than just one job with company X. If you were to say, 'You can only be attached to this company and you cannot have any other business interests,' as would be the case with Western businesses, you might find that you no longer have any employees."

John Hooker provides a good example: "An agent who favours personal friends is viewed as corrupt, because . . . it creates a conflict of interest:

a choice that is good for the agent and his or her cronies may not be good for the company." Whereas, in many parts of the world, "a purchasing agent does business with friends because friends can be trusted . . . It is assumed that cronies will follow through on the deal, not because they fear a lawsuit, but because they do not wish to sacrifice a valuable relationship in an economy where relationships are the key to business. In such a system, it is in the company's interest for the agent to do business with friends, and cronyism may, therefore, present no additional risk of exploitation or dishonesty."

The risk is that operating a system based on personal relationships can encourage those who do not have an established set of such relationships to buy them, perhaps through unethical practices such as bribery. While it is important to address any issues with consideration for local conduct and practice, it is also important to encourage behaviour consistent with the values of the organisation and the requirements of external regulations. It is therefore important to establish, for the benefit of both the business and the local workforce, the clear differences between personal business relationships and unethical business relationships.

There are practical considerations in implementing this approach. For example, carrying out due diligence checks on individuals can sometimes cause offence regardless of whether there is a suggestion of possible corruption, simply because it may be taken to suggest a lack of trust. As Bob Chandler explains, "The external investor has to be sensitive to the local environment, and work out a code of ethics where everyone discloses their other interests, and you have some framework which allows them to co-exist with their main employer. Then, you can better run the business." In other words, the key first step is in building sufficient buy-in from the local team to allow the business to form an accurate picture of the relationships that exist.

Furthermore, understanding and safeguarding relationships is not just an important issue for international investors dealing with a new culture. Fraud is often based on the abuse of trust, so operating in a business culture built around trust can present an opportunity for potential fraudsters. Bob Chandler says, "The whole issue of abuse of trust is a common feature in many cases. When employees and business partners are trusted, they are trusted completely; whereas in more developed markets, you tend to have grades of trust. You would seldom trust someone fully."

Community mix

One additional consideration in understanding the region's fraud risk is the composition of the population. This is characterised by a mix of nationalities, with many expatriates filling important roles, alongside local nationals. For example, at least 30% of the 13 million-strong population of the UAE, Bahrain, Oman and Qatar, are Indian. The composition of the workforce affects the business landscape and, therefore, also affects the fraud risks to which a business is exposed.

One challenge caused by operating in such a cosmopolitan environment is that communicating a clear, consistent tone can be more difficult. Bob Chandler explains that, "Because there is a mixture of cultures and established groups, unless you have an exceptionally good tone at the top, it is unlikely that information will filter through these different communities to the top decision-makers. It will only get so far, and you simply won't know about issues until after the event. Had you known about them and seen those red flags, maybe you could have stopped things."

Staff from countries which are independent of the established groups in multinational organisations can often be effective in communicating messages about the culture of the parent company and provide an "outside" or independent view of the prevailing business practices in the local business to the parent company. However, for the reasons already explained in relation to the different perceptions of business relationships, employees from outside the region may misinterpret the behaviour of their colleagues in the absence of appropriate training and induction. There is an important balance to be struck in relation to the diversity of the workforce.

In addition to this challenge, many businesses are now also witnessing a handover from the founding owners to the next generation of businessmen. These individuals will typically have been educated abroad and will have the confidence to run the business on their own, but may seek to run operations in a different way and inculcate a new style of management. The key for an investor is to understand dynamics of the local team, through personal interaction and appropriate due diligence.

Conclusion

Engaging in business in rapid growth markets including the four regions examined here requires understanding environments that are markedly different to those of the mature markets. However, what these markets all share is that they are anticipated to be tomorrow's economic growth engines.

In such an environment, where growth and development drive social and economic change, there is a huge range of opportunities for fraudsters to exploit. For example, significant disparities in the way data is held and shared, with a mix of manual and electronic systems, present an opportunity for those willing to exploit this information asymmetry and pose a risk to those willing to believe anything or turn a blind eye in the scramble for a return. While regulation and enforcement in these markets are becoming more prominent it inevitably responds to realities on the ground. For those investing in new areas, uncertainty and inexperience also mean a dependence on local advice and local contacts, creating a further area of risk.

So, whilst these markets bear a significant number of common features, it is clear that the differences between them mean that they cannot each be treated in the same way.

- Contracts: differences in the nature and enforceability of the contractual relationship are fundamental. Whilst this is changing to varying degrees across the regions, it is clear that those used to the rights and obligations of traditional contracts need to think differently about such matters.

- Information: those used to the ability to consult up to date, electronic databases on corporate entities and their ownership will be disheartened by the incompleteness and inaccessibility of the equivalent records in these markets. Whether it is the result of fronting in Africa or insufficient transparency in China, organisations will need to work harder to understand exactly who they are dealing with.

- Official corruption: in many rapid growth markets official corruption within governmental organisations remains an issue. Whilst certainly not unique to these regions, it is clear that organisations are more likely to encounter corrupt practices here than in the mature markets to which they are used. However, the situation is changing as legislative and enforcement activities are helping to deliver progress in dealing with the threats.

As with all new ventures, local experience is the key to helping organisations tap into the potential of these markets. In India, this will be needed to navigate the uniquely challenging bureaucracy, whilst in China, assistance might be required in understanding the complex relationships between individuals and companies. In Africa, procurement processes must be operated so that they not only deliver the best price, but also circumvent the collusion and manipulation that are often found in bidding and tendering processes. In the Middle East, understanding the balance between the value and risks associated with employees' external interests can represent a completely novel challenge.

As one commentator, Ginger Szala, explained during a discussion on the risks and opportunities in emerging markets, "The main lesson was to pay attention to details, to the players, rules and regulations and especially to current events. One manager noted two 'great stories' that changed overnight from an investment paradise to an investment nightmare: Egypt and Turkey. 'The last thing you want is your assets stuck in an affiliate overseas,' he said."[25]

Anti-corruption bribery & corruption due diligence: key questions

Merger and acquisition activity is on the rise in high risk, high growth countries. Many companies focus on financial due diligence to manage the investment risk – only to find that they have a bribery and corruption risk exposure post acquisition. Spotting the red flags early is dependent upon asking the right questions at an early stage:

- Are sales to government or state owned entities significant in the context of total sales?

- Are sales secured through intermediaries?

- Does the business require government authorisations (e.g., environment and other permits or licences) to operate in-country?

- Is the supply chain or corporate structure complex?

- Is the ownership structure complex or opaque?

- Is there a lack of financial statements or financial information?

- Is the companies' auditor unaccredited?

1. http://www.imf.org/external/index.htm

2. http://www.berkshirehathaway.com/letters/2001pdf.pdf

3. Ramalinga Raju, Letter to the Board of Directors, January 2009

4. The study, by ASK Investment Managers of Mumbai, shows that the five and 10-year compound annual growth of the top Indian entrepreneur-led firms was more than double the fastest-growing multinational corporations (MNC) and state-owned corporations (PSUs).

5. Supreme Court of India, 2 February 2012

6. http://cag.gov.in/html/reports/civil/2010-11_19PA/Telecommunication%20Report.pdf

7. http://cpi.transparency.org/cpi2012/

8. *Navigating Today's Complex Business Risks – Europe, Middle East, India and Africa Fraud Survey 2013*, EY

9. http://www.deccanherald.com/content/115453/cbi-busts-huge-fake-housing.html

10. http://articles.economictimes.indiatimes.com/2012-08-07/news/33083590_1_bank-fraud-public-sector-banks-cbi

11. Prabhakar, Binoy. "DLF-Vadra story: Why real estate in India has become synonymous with bribes & black money." *The Economic Times*, 15 October 2012, via Dow Jones Factiva

12. "Gradual Upturn in Global Growth During 2013," *World Economic Outlook Update*, IMF, 23 January 2013

13. "Africa rising" *The Economist*, 3 December 2011, http://www.economist.com/node/21541015 [Accessed 15/07/2013]

14. *Navigating Today's Complex Business Risks – Europe, Middle East, India and Africa Fraud Survey 2013*, EY

15. Moyo, Dambisa. "Why Foreign Aid Is Hurting Africa." *Wall Street Journal*, 21 March, 2009

16. http://www.fin24.com/Economy/State-moves-to-curb-BEE-fronting-20110612

17. Auty, Richard M. *Sustaining Development in Mineral Economies: The Resource Curse Thesis*. London: Routledge, 1993

18. "Nigeria fuel subsidy report 'reveals $6bn fraud." *BBC*, 24 April 2012

19. "PPPRA Increases Fuel Importers to over 40 Firms", This Day Live, 24 July 2013

20. http://eiti.org/document/progressreport

21. "CSRC head vows to get tough on financial crimes", China Daily, 2 August 2013

22. Wu, Mark. "Piercing China's Corporate Veil: Open Questions from the New Company Law". *The Yale Law Journal*. Volume 117. Number 2. November 2007. pp. 329-338

23. "SEC Charges China-Based Company and CEO in Latest Cross-Border Working Group Case" http://www.sec.gov/news/press/2013/2013-115.htm

24. http://www.mondaq.com/unitedstates/x/244996/Audit/PCAOB+Announces+Agreement+With+China+On+Production+Of+Audit+Work+Papers+A+Step+Forward+Or+Lip+Service

25. http://www.futuresmag.com/2013/06/26/beware-of-emerging-markets-and-other-things-that-g

Chapter 9

Cybercrime: A unique challenge?

Introduction

In the previous chapter, we considered the fraud landscape in different parts of the world – identifying distinctive factors that affect the nature of the risk in those regions. In many ways, the Internet is just another 'country' with its own set of unique opportunities and threats to which organisations must respond. But, whereas companies can choose whether to enter a new market, they have no choice when it comes to the Internet – they are already there, and they need to deal with the consequences right now.

What is cybercrime?

The ubiquity of the Internet and related technologies, such as email and online banking, enable a range of new fraud threats which present some unique challenges. But the issue is not just one of scale; it is also an issue of the rate of change. Criminals, including fraudsters, target vulnerabilities in organisations in transition, thus it is precisely at the moment when companies adapt to the technologies required to keep their businesses competitive that they are vulnerable. One expert observed, "The computer can be either a tool or a target for the fraudster[1]", and generally, it is both. Organisations are, therefore, struggling to continue to keep pace with the fraudster whose innovative use of the Internet and computing power to commit fraud is continuously evolving.

Almost any fraud can involve a computer at some juncture; but this does not make each such crime a 'cybercrime'. Definitions muddy the issue with one commentator, David S. Wall, preferring the term 'cyberspace crime'[2]. For our purposes we consider cybercrime and cyberfraud to be activity which is committed primarily through the use, or deliberate misuse, of computers and the Internet. More narrowly, Cyberfraud itself is further distinguished by the fact that it entails theft and deceit.

For a variety of reasons, the economic effect of cybercrime is hard to quantify with accuracy. Firstly, cybercrime is historically an underreported phenomenon. At the corporate level, in particular, there is a disincentive to admit to being a victim of cybercrime due to the fear of the consequential reputational damage, loss of consumer confidence and even copycat attacks that result from the associated adverse publicity[3]. Secondly, there are jurisdictional challenges to pursuing and prosecuting cybercriminals. Cybercrime can often take place on multiple servers across multiple jurisdictions, with the perpetrators located anywhere in the world; therefore where and with whom the responsibility for fighting cybercrime rests is a grey area. Furthermore, when a business suffers from reputational damage, it can take years to regain the lost ground. Given the nature of the consequences and difficulties in tracking down the perpetrators, it is no surprise that online crime "is not only a matter of prosecution, but also – and perhaps even more – a matter of prevention[4]."

Some incidents that have been reported in the media provide insight into the magnitude of the problem. Early media attention focused on incidents that were experienced by some of the large Internet businesses. A number of high profile websites, for example, were attacked by a group of hackers at the turn of the 21st century. The cybercriminals hacked into their systems and changed elements of their system coding. Websites were forced to shut down so that the organisations could stop the unauthorised activity, repair the damage and address the security flaws[5]. In the meantime, the business operations were either slowed down or halted altogether. Within only a few days of the attack, the share prices of the affected companies dropped by up to 9%[6].

More recently, cybercriminals have extended their reach beyond the front-end websites and deep into the organisations themselves. The targets are no longer restricted to Internet companies, instead extending to almost all industries and even governments. One recent high profile example from 2012 demonstrates the extent to which companies can be infiltrated – one of the world's largest companies, Saudi Aramco, was apparently targeted by hackers who managed to introduce a particularly infectious computer virus into the company's non-production systems. In a statement, Saudi Aramco indicated that about 30,000 of its workstations had been affected[7].

Despite the challenges, there have been a number of attempts to quantify the monetary impact of cybercrime. Europe-wide losses due to credit and debit card fraud, for example, have been put at €1.5bn in 2012[8], while the number of reported major attacks on large businesses and government rose 250-fold from just two major attacks a day in 2010 to 500 a day by 2012, with no sign of slowing down. One unfortunate UK business is reported to have lost £800m as a result of a single security breach. Europol, whilst acknowledging that it is hard to know the full costs of cybercrime, estimates the annual losses at $1trn[9].

A major systematic study into the true cost of cybercrime was commissioned by the UK Ministry of Defence (MoD) in 2012[10]. It found that the total annual cost of cybercrime, including that associated with the anti-cybercrime infrastructure in the UK, was almost $18bn. Of this, infrastructure accounted for over $700m. In worldwide terms, these figures were $225bn and $25bn, respectively and serve to show the magnitude of the cost of cybercrime, both to businesses and to the general public.

In addition to the very significant financial loss, the 'total cost' includes the value of stolen information and the costs of efforts associated with remediating compromised systems. Notwithstanding the challenges of accurate measurement, there is no doubt that this is a very significant and urgent problem which organisations need to confront if they wish to maintain the integrity and viability of their businesses.

Characteristics of cyberfraud

So, what is it about cyberfraud that demands a different approach to the counter-fraud strategies and tactics? In many ways, the end result of cyberfraud is little different to that of conventional fraud – the theft of something of value. It is simply a new means to the same end: 'old wine in new bottles,' as the saying goes.

An important aspect of cyberfraud that serves to differentiate some of the schemes, is the central role of 'social engineering' in its execution. Social engineering entails persuading people to divulge information that they would normally keep private or undertake actions that they would not ordinarily do. This is a necessary step in gaining access to, and control of, the target systems and assets. This might, for example, be to persuade the target to share a password or execute a particular combination of commands on a computer system with the ultimate aim of weakening the protection provided to the assets. Elsewhere, social engineering has been widely quoted as, "a non-technical kind of intrusion that relies heavily on human interaction and often involves tricking other people to break normal security procedures."

A person using social engineering to break into a computer network might try to gain the confidence of an authorised user and get them to reveal information that compromises the network's security. Social engineers often rely on the natural helpfulness of people, as well as on their weaknesses. They might, for example, call the employee describing some kind of urgent problem that requires immediate network access. Such techniques deliberately appeal to vanity, authority or greed of the target. Alternatively, old-fashioned eavesdropping is another typical social engineering technique.

One of the most infamous examples of the use of social engineering is in the execution of advance fee fraud or the 419 Letter (a reference to the part of the Nigerian criminal code violated by the fraud). This fraud relies upon the tendency for the prospect of a 'reward' to cloud the victim's rational judgement.

Such frauds have been perpetrated in postal and fax form for many decades but the growth of online technology makes their implementation much cheaper and opens up a much greater population of potential targets. The cyber version of this scam consists of the potential victim receiving an email purported to be from a former or current government official who tells of owning an immense fortune that cannot be removed from their bank account, perhaps due to a turbulent political situation. The fraudster claims to need funds or details of the victim's bank account to facilitate a bank transfer; in return, the potential victim is promised a share of the fortune. Of course, after getting what he needs, the fraudster disappears after taking the funds or emptying the victim's bank account. In fact, this fraud dates from as far back as the Anglo–Spanish war in the 16th century, where a 'Spanish nobleman' would fool an Englishman into believing that he was a political exile whose profoundly wealthy sister is being held prisoner and was in need of rescue[11].

The external threat

In contrast to traditional fraud, where the greatest threat is found within the organisation itself, the most significant threat of cybercrime comes from the outside. This is the result of a variety of factors – not least, the fact that the physical location of the criminal and his computer is almost completely irrelevant to the execution of the crime. Another factor is the widespread availability of the tools required to conduct cybercrime.

Anti-cybercrime defences need two forms of activity in their sights. A single cybercrime may not in itself present a serious threat to an organisation's security. However, it has been asserted by Wall that, "there is a long-standing lay person's expectation that cybercrimes are serious and dramatic, when in fact their main threat lies in their aggregation[12]". The largest attacks have the capacity to destroy a system or steal very large amounts of information or funds from a business, whilst small ones steal small quantities at a great rate. Their size and individual impact present a particular detection problem. Indeed, it is widely asserted that the biggest cybercrime danger is the gradual skimming of funds and personal data, particularly in the online realm, where millions of small transactions can be instigated using a few lines of computer code acting almost imperceptibly.

Two key techniques used by hackers to commit acts of cybercrime against organisations are the use of surveillance software, 'spyware', and the use of malicious software, known as 'malware'. Spyware ranges from low-level mass surveillance of activities to the use of a 'key-logger', which records everything that a target user types on their workstation. The latter can be very effective at gleaning user account details, passwords and other sensitive information. Spyware can be uploaded manually by a disgruntled employee, or it could also be unknowingly introduced to a network as a result of successful 'phishing'. One particularly imaginative technique provides an eye-opening insight into the ingenuity of these fraudsters. Under this devious scheme, a USB stick is dropped by the fraudster in the vicinity of the business that the fraudster would like to defraud. They then simply wait for a 'Good Samaritan' to plug it into their office computer, at which point a virus is released into the corporate network.

Malware takes many forms, with the common theme being the aim of causing some kind of damage or unauthorised activity. Trojan horse software, for example, is malware that is disguised as legitimate software; it is quite common for such Trojans to masquerade as computer security programs. In one incident, where cyberfraudsters had deployed a Trojan horse, an employee of a bank in South Africa could only watch as funds were moved out of his account as soon as he logged on to his computer.

Hacking crimeware kits for phishing and spoofing are readily available. No great technical knowledge is required to launch them at a defined target. One tool, Zeus software, which is commonly used by hackers is essentially a 'point-and-click' application reminiscent of mainstream business programs. The hackers do not have to code it to create a customised version of malware. The cybercriminals buy it from developers who sell it on underground forums.

The ubiquity of Internet access, powerful computing and illicit software opens up cyberfraud to a much wider universe of fraudster than any other crime. This in turn leads to a more diverse profile of cyberfraudsters. In their report mentioned above, Europol cites evidence that 60% of hackers are under the age of 25.

Such an inversion of skills and knowledge presents huge challenges to a generation of business leaders who were brought up in a different world.

The rise of state-sponsored cybercrime

One new threat that is receiving a great deal of attention is that of the state-sponsored attack. Whilst the exact details are unclear, evidence suggests that many states are involved to some extent. Some of the stories are, perhaps, unsurprising. For example, in July 2013, the South Korean government announced that it was allocating billions of dollars to counter the threat posed to its economy by North Korea's equally well-funded cyber-warfare unit.[13] In another widely reported case, the US is believed to have been responsible for deploying the highly sophisticated 'stuxnet' virus at the control systems of Iranium nuclear processing plants.[14]

The nature of the threat to individual organisations depends upon the sector. For those organisations whose value relies up on the development and exploitation of Intellectual Property, such as pharmaceutical companies or those in the high-technology industries, the target is likely to be their most valuable inventions. Such valuable secrets, gained through state-sponsored cyberespionage, may be used to provide a head-start to rapid-growth countries which do not already have such indigenous industries.

Another target may be the records of organisations who are engaged in tendering for large infrastructure contracts. Through penetrating their defences and gaining access to the details of bids, states can provide their own organisations with information that could assist them in undercutting competing bids and win the contracts unfairly.

Whilst in the previous examples, the objective of the intrusion is realised in the short term. There are other scenarios where the intrusion is aimed at deploying dormant agents which remain undetected until a time when they become useful – perhaps in the event of a change in political relations. This means that the infiltration will not be readily detectable – and neither will it be revealed through the results of the exploitation of stolen information.

A final example may be illustrated by the potential motives behind gaining access to companies engaged in software or hardware development. Obtaining details of future product developments will be an obvious objective, perhaps to identify weaknesses in security for example. A more subtle approach may be to introduce secret 'back-doors' into the code so that future users of the software may be compromised. Such information may then be sold to organisations around the world, fatally damaging the product's integrity from the very start.

So the threat to organisations of state-sponsored activity is potentially very serious. The risk of a state having access to all of its communications is significant. Dealing with that threat is certainly challenging and is likely to require significant external expertise if an organisation is to understand when it has been compromised, how it was compromised and how such an attack may be prevented in the future.

Insider risks

Whilst much of the focus, particularly in the media, is on the threat that emanates from external agents, the danger posed by either rogue or careless employees must not be ignored. A common motive for fraud is revenge; in particular if a potential fraudster has been overlooked for a promotion, or put on notice of disciplinary action or risk of redundancy. The significance of the threat from rogue employees is magnified by the fact that they have direct access to many, and sometimes all, of an organisation's internal systems.

This type of danger has been illustrated by a number of cases in which banking data for Swiss banks has been sold to tax authorities in Germany and several other European countries[15]. Insiders who also have the knowledge of cybercrime tools and techniques pose a very serious threat to their employers. However, the careless employee is, on the other hand, the target of social engineers who use phishing and spoofing to nullify corporate defences with malware or spyware. An email, purporting to be from their employer requesting login details, employee number or other sensitive information, gives the criminal the means to access the organisation's intranet. Access to confidential information also gives the criminal scope for blackmail and ultimately exposes the company to the risk of theft.

Reputational damage is a particular risk if it becomes public knowledge that an organisation has suffered an online security breach and this is particularly acute for sectors such as financial services or pharmaceuticals, where a reputation for safety and security is fundamental to the operation of the business.

All of this puts the onus on organisations to manage user accounts and the associated access levels actively. One of the best safeguards against cybercrimes is a strong password policy. Other approaches include monitoring the activity of such high-risk employees, and promptly disabling the accounts of individuals as they leave the organisation.

Dealing with the threat

Businesses do not need to reinvent the wheel to address the risk of cybercrime. Defence involves applying traditional anti-fraud techniques, but using new tools and considering the risks affecting new services. Cybercrime are, "manifested through incremental and *innovative* use of technology[16]", so the detection and prevention of cybercrime must also be innovative. The key to prevention is to regularly review and update business systems and safety measures as well as monitoring for unusual behaviours. The cybercriminals will constantly be looking for new ways to penetrate a business's systems, so those tasked with battling cybercrime must be looking at new ways to stop them. "Today, the technological cat-and-mouse game between offender and investigator remains much the same as in the past. Offenders still exploit new technologies, while the investigators catch up quickly and then use the same technologies for investigation, apprehension and prevention[17]." What is most startling is the speed at which the threats morph in response to the deployment of each successful prevention method.

Controls used by a company to prevent cybercrime must be innovative and, in many ways, use almost the same tools that are used to perpetrate cybercrimes. Companies can use their own versions of spyware and malware to monitor for suspicious activity that might be going on in their company. However, there can be a conflict between putting up defensive walls and ensuring ongoing business operations online. If an organisation does not get the balance right, it can either drive its customers away through overly onerous security, or leave itself open to attack by going too far the other way.

Alongside innovation, a company needs to pay heed to the mantra, 'Security is a process, not an event[18].' Due to the innovative nature of cybercrime, a business cannot expect to simply view the introduction of cybersecurity measures as a one-off occurrence. A security system that seems to be adequate one month can be broken into with relative ease the next. There needs to be an ongoing process of evaluation and review: "Corporations that treat security as a checkbox and fail to go above and beyond will be drastically limited in their ability in providing reasonable safeguards to protect their critical assets[19]."

The target of the cybercriminal is often user details and associated passwords. In response, the use of multiple levels of access can minimise the threat. Businesses often hold large volumes of client and customer personal data which employees access with a unique password. However, it is easier to attack a person than it is to hack a computer. One key precaution against such a break-in is the use of a system of 'multi-level access'. This ensures that the hacking of one person does not inevitably lead to a business's private data or funds being completely compromised. This is not, therefore, a technological problem – rather, protection may be achieved through continuous diligence in ensuring that users have no greater access rights more than is required to fulfil their roles.

Given the risks exposed by social engineering, an ethical business culture is also key to preventing cybercrime attacks. Firstly, the success of a cybercriminal or hacker increases exponentially with his knowledge and familiarity with the workings of a company. The weaker the company's relationship with its employees, the more likely the fraudster will find an 'inside man' who can provide their passwords or be willing to install some malware on to the company's systems. A company with a weak compliance culture is far less likely to see security as a process. Education is essential for maintaining security, and this needs to be conducted across the entire company and regularly refreshed to take into account emerging cybercrime and cyberfraud schemes.

Surveillance is another valuable element of defence. For example, emails may be monitored to prevent suspicious messages from reaching employees' mailboxes. In addition, such email traffic may also be monitored for high-risk key words that could trigger the alarm. This monitoring could also look for suspicious and out-of-context number combinations, such as account numbers or pass codes. Web security tools can also be deployed to prevent access to high-risk websites.

Because cybercrime is an omnipresent threat, constant monitoring is particularly important. Organisations are especially vulnerable out of normal business hours, at weekends and during holiday periods, when surveillance is at its lowest. In this respect, the rules of the real world apply equally to those of cyberspace.

Furthermore, companies need proactively to investigate their computer networks to identify if they may have already been compromised. Investigators often find that whilst investigating one incident, they uncover many more to which the victim organisation had been oblivious. This could be averted if organisations take a more rigorous approach to security. The focus needs to shift from assuming it has not been hacked and working to bolster your fortifications, to assuming it has been hacked and spending time looking for evidence of existing data theft.

In short, there is no 'silver bullet' solution or security product that will prevent cyberattacks. One estimate suggests that 20% of such incidents are unknown, although in reality the real figure could be much higher than this as most companies do not have the capability or staff to either identify or prevent cyberattacks[20]. This is why it is so important to understand cybersecurity as a process. "The UK National Audit Office report published in 2013[21] found that it will take up to 20 years to redress the skills shortage in the cybersecurity market. At the same time, whilst organisations work to address the skills gap, there has also been a change in the modus operandi of attacks – so there's no big event that tips off a company that it has been breached. Hackers are staying quiet – slowly accumulating data over years – seeking to sell it on, rather than defacing websites or maliciously publishing confidential data on forums."

The introduction of anti-cybercrime measures comes with a cost, both in financial terms – they have to be developed and introduced into systems – and in terms of application and customer obligation. The scale of the cost and the threat determines the strength of the defence erected around a company's IT system and its customers. The more valuable the assest under threat, and the greater the risk of penetration, the more comprehensive the anti-fraud measure. Companies will always live with the fear that they are behind the curve in terms of the latest cybercrime device or technique. "Don't think you can completely secure your IT estate with a massive wall. You have to take an intelligent approach: have a big wall around your crown jewels, but, everywhere else you [must] have installed CCTV, because you are not going to stop someone getting into your network. If they want to get in, they will."

The conclusion is that a flexible system of 'best practice' anti-cyber-crime measures for both government and industry is essential[22]. But businesses need also to rely on their own systems of prevention and detection. Across all organisations, governments and banks have done most work in the area of operational risk and these may be sources of guidance for corporate organisations with cyber concerns. Another source of information is the newly formed European Cybercrime Centre (EC3) created in January 2013.

It is important to maintain an international collaborative network between public and private sectors. These networks are absolutely key in a number of respects; in dissemination of information about the latest cyberattacks and in bringing international hacker and cybercrime rings to justice. This was shown in January 2013, when a number of Romanian cyberfraudsters were brought to justice for conspiracy to hack into hundreds of US-based computers to steal credit, debit and payment account numbers and associated data that belonged to US cardholders[23]. The case was reportedly investigated not only by the US Secret Service and the New Hampshire State Police, but also by the Romanian Directorate of Investigation of Organized Crime and Terrorism.

The seriousness of the threat is also illustrated by the hacking of the NASDAQ market in early 2011, which gave rise to concern that the hack-ers were motivated by "unlawful financial gain, theft of trade secrets and a national-security threat designed to damage the exchange[24]". The hackers had installed malware that allowed them to spy on many leading company directors who had logged on to directorsdesk.com. They were able to spy on scores of directors before the malware could be removed[25]. In the wake of the NASDAQ case, General Keith Alexander, head of the National Security Agency (NSA) and US Cyber Command, confirmed that the NSA was working with NASDAQ to improve their cybersecurity and help prevent any further attacks. A deeper working relationship between governments and the business community in the prevention of cybercrime will aid the fight against cyberattacks.

Despite the complexities and nuance of cybercrime with high-quality systems and a strong business culture, it need not present a significantly greater challenge than any other fraud risk. One commentator advised, "Just remember three key concepts about information security: people, process and technology. In addressing each of these categories diligently, you will reduce your risk posture and make the internet a lot safer for you to conduct business, adopt new business models with confidence and compete on a global level with a much higher level of security efficacy[26]." Winning the IT battle with fraudsters to minimise losses is no less critical than winning against your competitors to maintain and grow a profitable business.

Lessons from financial services

The financial services sector, both institutions and their customers, has long been the target of cybercriminals. This reflects both the size and liquidity of the target assets and the speed and enthusiasm with which the industry has embraced new technologies to make organisations leaner and more customer focused. This also reflects the reality that it is very difficult to create a fake high-street bank and make it look real enough to attract customers. On the other hand, it is much easier to create a convincing fake bank website.

Banks report that their customers are regularly targeted by hackers using phishing scams. Fraudsters who have obtained email addresses distribute a notice to a very large number of recipients saying that some suspicious activity has occurred on the account and it has been suspended. The recipient is told that he must confirm his identity by providing account details and other sensitive information in order to reactivate the account. A link in the email directs the user to an often convincing fake website into which he must enter the details, at which point the information enters the hands of the fraudsters.

Spear-phishers use the same technique of sending deceptive emails, but in such cases, the fraudsters make their opening gambit more tailored to the target, to add credibility, by extracting readily available information from social media sites.

The consequences of this type of cyberfraud are both financial liability and reputational damage. The best defence is robust protection of bank websites and bank data, and the education of customers, with clear guidance on the company's website that explains the dangers of online fraud and the need to report suspicious behaviour.

The industry continues to innovate in order to combat the growing power of the cyberfraudster. Such developments include:

- Innovations in user-authentication techniques, such as the use of biometrics and digital signatures. An example of this is the 'secure key', such as that introduced by HSBC in 2011[27].

- The use of web traffic analysis and visitor profiling. This aims to alert online monitors to suspicious or fraudulent activity.

- Schemes for website certification and endorsement. This will, in theory, make it more difficult to 'spoof' websites, although these still require a level of user-education that may be difficult to achieve in practice.

The implementation of security devices inevitably makes demands on customers, and banks cannot always rely on their cooperation. So, when HSBC introduced its secure key, there were reports of customer dissatisfaction[28]. Customers were reported to question the efficiency of the new system, and one was quoted as saying, "It was a lot of hassle to get it up and running. I tend to look at my account at work, but I won't do that now. I don't want to carry the device around and end up losing it. It means online banking isn't quite so straightforward and quick any more, which is a shame."

Conclusion

So, as with the challenge of operating in the emerging markets, working in cyberspace is really a matter of appreciating that it is not simply a case of business as usual. Rather, if the significant opportunities are to be exploited organisations must reassess the threats that they face and seek expertise to help to mitigate them.

1. David Porter of Resilient Thinking

2. Wall, David S. *Cybercrime: The Transformation of Crime in the Information Age.* Cambridge: Polity, 2007

3. Wall, 2007

4. Koops, Bert-Jaap and Ronald Leenes, "Identity Theft, Identity Fraud, and/or Identity-related Crime. Definitions Matter." *Datenshutz und Datensicherheit*, vol. 30, no. 9, p.555

5. Smith, Katherine T. Murphy L. Smith, Jacob L. Smith, "Case studies of cybercrime and their impact on marketing activity and shareholder value." *Academy of Marketing Studies Journal*, vol. 15, no. 2, 2011, pp.67–81

6. Ibid.

7. *"Saudi Aramco restores network services"*, company website

8. Glenny, Misha. "The battle against cybercrime is too important to be undone by Eurosceptics." http://www. guardian.co.uk/commentisfree/2013/jan/13/battle-against-cybercrime-eurosceptics?INTCMP=SRCH [Accessed, 15/07/2013]

9. *Threat Assessment (Abridged): Internet Facilitated Organised Crime.* https://www.europol.europa.eu/sites/ default/files/publications/iocta_0.pdf, EUROPOL Public Information

10. Anderson, R., C. Barton, R. Böhme, R. Clayton, M.J.G. van Eeten, M. Levi, T. Moore and S. Savage, "Measuring the Cost of Cybercrime" in *11th Workshop on the Economics of Information Security,* June 2012

11. Yar, Majid. *Cybercrime and Society*, Athenaeum, SAGE, London, 2006

12. Wall, 2007

13. *"South Korea Beefs up Cyber Security"*, Security Week, 4 July 2013

14. *"US was 'key player in cyber-attacks on Iran's nuclear programme'"*, The Guardian, 1 June 2012

15. "Switzerland charges man with selling bank's client data to Germany", Reuters, 28 June 2013

16. McQuade, Sam. "Technology-enabled Crime, Policing and Security." *Journal of Technology Studies*, vol. 32, no. 1, 2006

17. Wall, 2007

18. Chuvakin, Anton and Branden R. Williams. *PCI Compliance: Understand and Implement Effective PCI Data Security Standard Compliance.* Waltham: Syngress, 2012

19. Gragido, Will and John Pirc. *Cybercrime and Espionage: An Analysis of Subversive Multi-vector Threats.* Rockland: Syngress, 2011

20. Gragido and Pirc, 2011

21. *The UK cyber security strategy: Landscape review*, published by National Audit Office, 12 February 2013

22. Berkowitz, Bruce and Hahn, Robert W. "Cybersecurity: Who's Watching the Store?" *Issues in Science and Technology*, vol. 19, no. 3

23. Department of Justice: "Office of Public Affairs. Romanian National Sentenced to 21 Months in Prison for Role in Multimillion-Dollar Scheme to Remotely Hack into and Steal Payment Card Data from Hundreds of U.S. Merchants' Computers." http://www.justice.gov/opa/pr/2013/January/13-crm-028.html [Accessed, 15/07/2013]

24. Barrett, Devlin. "Hackers Penetrate Nasdaq Computers." http://online.wsj.com/article/SB10001424052748704709304576124502351634690.html?mod=WSJ_hp_LEFTTopStories

25. Finkle, Jim. "Exclusive: Nasdaq hackers spied on company boards." http://www.reuters.com/article/2011/10/20/us-nasdaq-hacking-idUSTRE79J84T20111020

26. Gragido and Pirc, 2011

27. The 'secure key' uses a formula that generates a code every time the HSBC customer uses the online banking facility. This code, which includes the time it was generated, is then checked against numbers created through an identical formula held on the internal HSBC system. Provided the numbers match up, customers are able to log in to the system.

28. See, for example, Jo Thornhill. "HSBC customers hit out at extra security as 'key' makes internet banking too slow." http://www.thisismoney.co.uk/money/saving/article-2025682/HSBC-customers-complain-extra-security-calculator-key-online-banking.html

Chapter 10

The future of fraud

Introduction

When we think of fraud and the issues surrounding it, of the myriad challenges, perhaps the greatest is to anticipate what the future holds so that we may make the right decisions to manage the changing threat. What will fraud look like in 10, 20 years or further into the future? What are the extraordinary frauds that are taking place right now that we will only discover in the future when so much damage has been done that they can no longer be sustained or disguised? What will the ordinary fraudster be up to? Mahatma Gandhi said, "The future depends on what we do today"[1]. In this chapter, we set out ideas to help you to take a fresh look at your organisation, the people that you deal with and the wider environment through a 'fraud lens', and prioritise anti-fraud activities today in the light of emerging fraud risks.

What has been will be again; what has been done will be done again . . .

Is there really nothing new under the sun? The roots of apparently new fraud schemes may be traced back through time to remarkably similar deceptions. The present day advance fee/419 letter fraud is just the modern version of similar scams conducted hundreds of years ago; the difference is the way in which advances, including those in communication, have changed the method of execution and increased the size of the pool of potential victims. Charles Ponzi's eponymous fraud was uncovered in the 1920s, and was itself an echo of Dickensian plot lines[2]. Tales of Troy's deception by the infamous Greek horse date back several thousand years before the discovery of the electron, let alone the creation of the computer virus. And perhaps this is not particularly surprising when we think again about the dictionary definition of fraud, which is eternally relevant:

> *Fraud: criminal deception; the use of false representations to gain an unjust advantage*[3].

Fraud is, as we have discussed throughout the book, all about people: a human perpetrator deceiving human victims. More than 15 years ago, the ACFE created a classification system for occupational fraud which remains relevant today[4]. In this model, they suggested that such fraud boils down into three categories – corruption, asset misappropriation and fraudulent statements. The essence of all three is that value (funds, assets, etc.) is extracted by the perpetrators from an employer, another party or the financial market and its participants.

If fraud is a fundamental constant, to understand how it is likely to change in the future, we need to look at forces that are likely to transform the world over coming decades. In relation to each factor, it is necessary to consider a few important aspects. How will each impact on the nature of the fraud and the identity of the fraudster? What will change in terms of the detection, investigation and recovery strategies? Is whistleblowing going to be made more or less likely as a result of regulatory activity? And who will be the victims – new segments of the population, new industries or new institutions?

Does the past provide the answers?

If, as we suggest, the essence of fraud was, is and always will be the same, then taking a look at ordinary and extraordinary frauds from the recent past is likely to provide some helpful guidance on how the elemental frauds have been shaped by human progress. Looking back to the time before the discovery of the extraordinary frauds at Enron, by Maxwell and others with which such names will forever be associated, were there any distinguishing signs that foretold of the impending disaster?

A few fraud facts

- Polly Peck, Maxwell Communications and WorldCom were led by flamboyant and dominant individuals who suborned others to implement their frauds.

- The corporations were grown out of small, relatively inconsequential companies. Enron, for example, started as a small, regional energy company. They were transformed into truly extraordinary organisations which dominated their markets and completed huge, often record-breaking acquisitions.

- Enron's peak market capitalisation in August 2000 was $60bn whilst WorldCom's value touched $186bn in the period before its collapse.

- Stanford and Madoff promised, and apparently effortlessly delivered, extraordinarily consistent and market-leading returns to investors. Instead, Stanford's business amounted to a fraud of up to $8bn whilst Madoff's victims found that over $60bn was missing.

- Enron's growth and profile was lauded by the media, politicians and investors alike. One article from April 2000[5], typical of the time, contains effusive praise for the company's 'innovation' and 'success'. This was little more than 18 months before Enron's bankruptcy.

So, perhaps it is significant that such extraordinary frauds were preceded by extraordinary tales of success and, in some cases, a large pool of potentially gullible, greedy and unquestioning victims. This does not mean that that every 'success' is a fraud in progress, just waiting to be detected. But, we can see that viewing such extraordinary performance with a more sceptical eye might just identify the impending disaster.

The relentless march of technology

One fact that we can be confident of is that advances in technology will continue to shape our world and the way we conduct our personal and professional lives. New business models will be created, whilst others will have passed their expiry date, rendered obsolete by some new break-through. Such changes present opportunities that fraudsters will inevitably exploit, but also give organisations new ways to fight back.

The fraudster

In thinking about what this means in terms of the identity of the fraud-ster, we reflect on the perspective from India of a trend towards the younger fraudster in line with the broader population profile. Such a trend may reflect an increasing disparity in the knowledge of an organi-sation's leaders in some areas, for example use of technology, and those lower down the chain of command. In the home, children and teenag-ers are the ones who are teaching their parents how to properly use the gadgets and technologies that are becoming part of their lives. Such an asymmetry of knowledge has the potential to be exploited for illicit, as well as legitimate, purposes

So, if the fraudster does become younger, previous assumptions that inform the management of fraud risks will need to be reassessed. New frauds are likely to emerge as this new generation of fraudsters aban-dons the constraints of traditional thinking. In response, perhaps this will also mean that the profile and skills of the fraud investigator will change to reflect areas of vulnerability and asymmetry of knowledge

Detection

As fraudsters are becoming better armed, similar advances in technol-ogy provide organisations with novel means to defend themselves. We have seen, for example, that the increasing volumes of data generated by day-to-day operations provide raw material for the application of more advanced analysis, utilising the greater processing power that is routinely available. This is likely to include the automated analysis of voice recordings.

An initiative that is exploiting the proliferation of routinely generated data is being led by the SEC as they increase the focus on fraudulent financial reporting. Their Center for Risk and Quantitative Analysis has developed the Accounting Quality Model (AQM) which was swiftly given the name "Robocop" by the financial press[6]. In summary, the AQM is designed to exploit the increased use of XBRL, a system by which companies file reports in a standardised electronic format. These XBRL reports can be swiftly ingested into the analytical framework so that they can be subjected to a barrage of tests to identify those financial statements which appear suspicious.

These tests include the assessment of the accounting judgements made by the company and even the narrative sections of the reports to identify language which is similar to that of known fraudulent reports. Combining these and other analysis with comparisons of the company's peers, the objective of the model is to direct the attention of the SEC's enforcement team within hours of filing being made. These are early days for this type of monitoring, but given the level of attention that it is receiving, it is likely to be an area that will continue to rapidly develop particularly as the use of XBRL becomes much more pervasive.

Another area, however, that is likely to see an even larger leap forward is the assimilation and analysis of the data that resides outside the organisation – in online journals, blogs and other social media websites. As such material proliferates and individuals live more of their lives in the online world – and share their thoughts in this altogether more public forum – this external information may provide early warning signs.

Investigation and asset tracing

Tracing funds that have been stolen or assets that have been paid for with such funds can be a laborious process. Technology continues to make such efforts a little easier as the databases that contain relevant information become much more accessible and searchable. This is supplemented by increased international efforts in relation to improving transparency and openness – for example, offshore banks are no longer the safe haven that they once represented for the world's fraudsters and money launderers.

One additional, perhaps more transformative, effect of such technological change is a consequence of the same factors mentioned in the context of detection – the burgeoning world of social media. Unguarded comments posted by individuals in this domain may point to valuable assets, which the investigators can target for recovery. Looking further forward, the increased prevalence of geocoding, the embedding of GPS-driven location details into photographs, will further add to the precision with which assets may be identified and located.

Virtual currencies

If tracing funds through bank accounts across many jurisdictions is difficult, imagine the greater challenge where the funds have been converted into a currency that is outside of the control of any physical country. Such currencies, often referred to as alt-currencies, are now emerging with names such as Bitcoin, Litecoin, Feathercoin and Freicoin. These are starting to receive official recognition – in Germany, for example, gaining the status of a 'unit of account' so that they can be used for private transactions.

The potential of such currencies to transform the nature of fraud and the ability of fraudsters to hide their ill-gotten gains is mind-boggling, as a recent article illustrates[7]: "If Bitcoin, or a currency working in a similar way to it, got a stable value and a large user base, it could take cash flows forever out of the hands of government. Whether that's a great thing or a terrible thing depends on what you're trying to do, what you think of government and what country you're talking about."

The consequences of persistence

One of the unpleasant facts facing millions of people worldwide is that their past, as recorded in Tweets, Facebook entries and the like, simply persists in the ether. The same applies to media stories, press releases from regulators and professional bodies and other official records, such as court judgments. Historically, these records have been available to organisations in one form or another, although the onward march of technology has made access much easier and quicker, and widened the range of sources. Such information is available to all – irrespective of where in the world they are located.

This permanence of information is a blessing for would-be investigators and asset tracers, but it is also likely to be a curse for those individuals who have transgressed in the past and have been apprehended. In view of the increasing availability of databases, and archived press reports, the days of the serial fraudster who relies upon hiding his past and reoffending may be numbered – at least without reinventing or stealing a whole new identity each time.

This leads us to suggest that the seriousness and long-lasting consequences of being caught and punished are likely to represent an increasing deterrent for the wavering fraudster.

Changing demographics

In the context of technology innovation, we have seen that there may be consequences for future frauds as a result of disparities in the distribution of skills and knowledge of the different generations. There are other factors, demographic and social in nature, which are likely to impact on the identity of the fraudster, the victim and the nature of the crimes that might be committed.

The middle classes

The middle classes in the mature and rapid-growth markets appear to be taking diametrically opposed paths. In the mature markets, the middle class seems to be shrinking as populations polarise at the rich and poor extremes of the scale. Job insecurity afflicts many who, in the past, would enjoy long careers in previously stable industries. In concert with this, salaries are being eroded, fringe benefits cut and pensions are becoming both more expensive and less generous. In rapid-growth markets, the middle classes are growing, upward mobility being fuelled by growth at home and increasing demand from overseas markets.

This is significant because, as we have seen, historically, both surveys and anecdotal evidence have pinpointed the trusted middle manager as the most likely perpetrator of corporate fraud. We have also seen that periods of transition present both the opportunity and motivation for fraudulent acts.

Those under increasing pressure in the developed world, who are facing declining living standards whilst they perceive the upper echelons of society getting richer, are more likely to feel entitled to steal what is not theirs. In such conditions, we believe the threats from within can only grow.

In contrast, those in the developing world are experiencing what will feel like meteoric progress. Their expectations may accelerate beyond what is legitimately achievable, and they may turn to fraudulent means to close the gap. The acknowledged shortage in such markets of the availability of appropriately skilled managers may also result in an increase in the opportunity for fraud.

Ageing populations

The phenomenon of ageing populations affects many parts of the world as declining birth rates combine with advances in health care. Such a significant structural change in the population is likely to have an impact on the nature of fraud.

On one hand, the retirement of a generation of experienced managers and leaders may leave gaps in the 'corporate memory', which may be exploited by fraudsters. Equally, a growing pool of relatively wealthy, but ageing, individuals may give rise to a new wave of scams (such as the misselling of products and services) that exploit their vulnerability to target their assets.

Remote interactions

One of the often-suggested deterrents to fraud relates to the loyalty that is felt between individuals within a team and the way in which fraudsters cannot simply perceive their frauds as 'victimless'. Members of the team do not want to be seen to 'let the rest down'. Such a team spirit is generated by close working and overall association with a set of shared values – including those of the organisation that employs them.

This 'team spirit' maybe under threat from what is currently widely treated as a benign practice – flexible working. Through a variety of innovations and practices, this has the effect of employees spending more time working remotely – often at home – and at times that are more compatible with their lifestyles and personal commitments. This has many proven benefits, but one negative consequence may be the weakening of the important bonds of loyalty and team spirit, thus diminishing one of the deterrents to fraud.

This effect may also be seen to interact with another emerging practice – the 'zero hour contracts', under which employers do not guarantee a set number of hours of work. The apparently overt asymmetry in the balance of the employment relationship that this embodies may further erode the loyalty that employees feel to their employers.

The evolution of leadership

As we have seen, the nature of an organisation's leadership has a very significant role in the management of fraud risk. Leaders are expected to set the tone of their organisations. They are also likely to have the perspective and experience to identify behaviours and performance that seems to be 'not quite right'. On the other side, those leaders with malign intent use their power and status to perpetrate fraudulent activity. It therefore follows that the way in which the nature of leadership evolves may have an impact on the way fraud risk develops in the future.

Gender

Women are gaining increasing representation in more senior management and board positions. One of the most obvious features of the frauds that we have discussed throughout this book is that they have predominantly been formulated and executed by men. The famous female fraudster is rare. One of the reasons for this is the fact that, in the past, few women have been in the positions of power that have provided the opportunity for 'extraordinary frauds'. But what if that apparent barrier was removed – would this mean more or fewer frauds?

There is currently little evidence to help us to anticipate the impact of the greater representation of women in the boardroom. Will their presence increase the level of scrutiny? In the case of Enron and WorldCom, the whistleblowers were women but it remains to be seen in the longterm how their presence in the boardroom impacts corporate behaviour.

In terms of more scientific research, one interesting report by Transparency International (TI) suggested significant differences between the number of male and female whistleblowers[8]. In their study, TI found that, across all regions, women consistently represented a minority of whistleblowers. TI did not posit any significant conclusions, and many factors are likely to influence such behaviours, including the relative representation of men and women in positions where they might observe fraudulent activity and the possibility that they may be more susceptible to stay quiet when they do. However, if it is true that in general, women are less likely to use current whistleblowing channels, it poses challenges to the design and implementation of whistleblowing facilities for the changing workforce.

The itinerant CEO?

A visible trend in recent years has been the reducing tenure of chief executives at leading organisations. In the past, leaders would emerge from the ranks, having been immersed in the culture of the organisation, ready to pick up the baton handed to them by the previous, long-standing leader; and so the pattern continued from generation to generation. Increasingly, it seems that some such leaders are selected from outside of the organisation, often from entirely different industries or cultures, recognising, perhaps, the benefits that different perspectives bring to the organisation's strategy. In addition, they tend to remain in post for shorter periods of time, moving on to the next organisation. What does this change mean in the context of the future of fraud?

We would argue that this potentially has both positive and negative implications in relation to fraud. A new leader with a fresh mandate may be free to challenge things that have been put in place under the previous incumbent. They will be in an ideal position to view the organisation through fresh eyes and challenge established behaviours that undermine it or identify the inconsistencies that very often point to fraud. Further, historically, it has not been often that a leader enters an organisation and immediately turns it down a fraudulent path – the leaders that we have examined in this book had been long standing, inextricably associated with the organisations they subverted.

The counter to this argument is that the insecurity of the position of the leader could, in fact, act against this potentially idealist view. If their position is uncertain, is it really likely that they will challenge the vested interests of those with the power to undermine or fire them? And, even if they sought to make changes, a deep-seated culture is almost impossible to realign through a simple replacement of leader. Beyond this, such insecurity may also resonate with a workforce that is already feeling the adverse effects of economic weakness on their own job security. How loyal will they feel to an organisation which appears to change even its most senior people so readily?

Follow the money

An alternative way of thinking about where fraud is most likely to rear its head in the future is through seeking to identify the potential targets – the emerging pockets of value. Such an approach of 'following the money', a phrase itself inextricably associated with the Watergate scandal of the 1970s, may help us to consider the direction in which fraud could be heading.

We can illustrate this in the context of financial statement fraud. In the 1980s, the focus of financial statement manipulation was often associated with the opportunities provided by the relatively flexible rules around merger accounting. Under these rules, it was possible to exploit 'big bath' provisions and goodwill to portray more favourable corporate performance, particularly in the context of achieving reported growth through acquisition. In his then controversial book, *Accounting for Growth: Stripping the Camouflage from Company Accounts*, Terry Smith exposed these and other accounting tricks and techniques, most of which were subsequently rendered obsolete through changes to accounting standards.

The motivation for such behaviour was in the image and status this gave the corporate giants that led these companies from takeover to takeover – often needing to do so simply to maintain the illusion of success. The case of Polly Peck represents an example of this. As times moved on and such 'accounting' opportunities were systematically closed down, the focus turned to the link between share prices and executive rewards, which was being created by increasingly lucrative share-based remuneration.

The need to maintain consistent, reliable growth in profits and other measures of performance is driven by the fact that this is richly rewarded by the market in the form of concomitant share price progression. Such financial performance may be achieved through the manipulation of the more judgemental numbers that appear within an organisation's financial statements – provisions, accruals and deferrals, which are supposed to represent management's best estimate of future expenses or revenues. Many schemes have been discovered that entail the highly organised creation of artificial financial reporting outcomes and the posting of the necessary financial journals to deliver such results. The companies where such manipulations have been discovered often pay a significant price. Expensive and disruptive investigations are often followed by multi-million Euro fines. The necessary public restatements of financial results can also have detrimental impact on the share price and may leave the organisation vulnerable to a take over.

In recent public announcements, the SEC has stated that it will be bringing its focus back to such financial statement fraud with the establishment of a 'Fraud Task Force' which will use the outputs of the AQM mentioned earlier in this chapter[9].

Beyond such schemes, other tricks have been used to increase the value of share-based remuneration. Perhaps the most significant of these were the option backdating scandals, whereby the issue price of share options was manipulated by backdating the issue date. The effect was to increase the value of the share options to the recipient executives through a reduction in the cost of exercising the options. This was found to extend to a very large number of mainly US corporations, some of which were extremely high profile – at Brocade Communications, for example, it was reported that the discovery and subsequent restatements resulted in an increase in expenses of over $700m[10].

But what is next, where are the new targets for such frauds? Where are the numbers likely to be big enough to mask the manipulations? In our view, the potential areas include some of the following:

Pension funds

For many organisations, the impact of the performance of their pension funds on their finances can be significant. Investments returns are decreasing just as life expectancy in almost every country is increasing. This perfect storm is weighing heavily on organisations that are already struggling against the headwinds of an economic downturn.

Organisations may, therefore be turning to innovative techniques to maintain the value of the pension funds without further weakening their own financial position. Such solutions illustrate the ingenuity of the legitimate devices that are being used to deal with a very real and urgent problem. It does not take a huge leap of the imagination to contemplate how unscrupulous management could devise extraordinary schemes to commit acts of fraud.

Sustainability and integrated reporting

Over the next decade, the way in which companies may choose to report their performance will be transformed by the increasing use of integrated reports. The main principle behind this change is that a more complete assessment of a company's business performance can be achieved through understanding the wider impact of the company's activities on the outside world and the resources and relationships that sustain it. This is also consistent with other initiatives which are promoting a 'fair, balanced and understandable' approach to company reporting.

The potential value of such reporting is significant – providing the investor and market with a much better basis for understanding the long-term prospects for sustainability of the company's performance. But, as we have seen before, circumstances of transition present opportunities for the unscrupulous to take advantage. If, as is expected, the information within such reports becomes a focus for the markets (or other significant decision-makers, such as governments or even procurement directors) and positive reports result in more favourable treatment, there is the potential for inappropriate activity, such as the dishonest manipulation of results, to take place. If this happens, then the challenge of detection will be significant as there will be little experience of what is 'normal' performance.

A shift in responsibility?

Identifying, with certainty, the source and nature of future fraud threats is almost impossible. But there is one development that makes addressing this challenge more critical for organisations: the increasing trend that we discussed in Chapter 7 for governments to introduce legislation which places explicit responsibilities for corporates to fight fraud and corruption. The mechanisms for this are illustrated by the measures within anti-bribery laws, which imposes strict liability on organisations whose employees have been found paying bribes. The defence to this is that the company employed 'adequate procedures' to deal with this risk. Similar instances of corporate culpability are found throughout the world, including, for example, in the area of cartels and anti-competitive behaviour.

Whilst this trend tells us little about precisely where corporate fraud is heading, it sends a clear message that, in the future, more and more responsibility to deal with it will rest explicitly with the private sector.

In turn, this means that individual executives have even more personal responsibility for the conduct of the company and its employees than ever before. Sending fraud and corruption risk to the top of the boardroom agenda.

A final thought

As we have seen, one of the most recent fundamental drivers of change has been hyper-innovation, which essentially began with the invention of the microchip 40 years ago. This has transformed many aspects of people's lives – in previously unimaginable ways. If we were to look beyond the time span considered in this chapter to 30 or 40 years into the future, would we see a similarly 'science fiction-like' transformation?

Consider just one aspect of technological change – the relentless increase in the processing power of computers. Forty years ago, the electronic calculator was a rare sight, whilst PCs were almost unheard of. And yet, in June 2013, it was announced that a university in China had developed the fastest supercomputer yet. With the capacity of more than 300 million personal computers the Tianhe-2 has the ability to perform more than 33 thousand trillion calculations each second[11]. This presents a picture of massive processing power.

Fast forward another 30 or 40 years. What might we see then? What impact would unimaginable computing power have on fraud? In terms of fraud detection, we could see advanced systems that could detect and even anticipate fraudulent activity in ways that exceed today's most sophisticated algorithms. But we have seen that such advances also better equip the fraudster or, perhaps, even rogue computers, which might be able to design and execute frauds with minimal human intervention.

And one thing is for sure, the way in which old and new fraud schemes are perpetrated, detected and investigated will be very different in the future – even if the fundamental essence of fraud remains constant.

1. Mahatma Gandhi

2. Dickens, Charles. *Little Dorrit* (1857) and *Martin Chuzzlewit* (1844)

3. *The Concise Oxford Dictionary*

4. *1996 Report to the Nation on Occupational Fraud and Abuse*. Copyright 2006 by the Association of Certified Fraud Examiners, Inc.

5. "The Power Merchant [ENRON, NO. 18] Once a dull-as-methane utility, Enron has grown rich-making markets where markets were never made before." *Fortune Magazine*, 17 April 2000

6. "SEC to roll out 'RoboCop' against fraud", *Financial Times*, 13 February 2013

7. http://www.guardian.co.uk/commentisfree/2013/may/30/bitcoin-beyond-reach-of-government?INTCMP=SRCH

8. *"Why do women report corruption less than men?"* Transparency International, 8 March 2013

9. "Financial Reporting and Accounting Fraud", a speech by Andrew Ceresney, Co-Director of Enforcement, US SEC on 19 September 2013

10. Smith, T. *Accounting for Growth: Stripping the Camouflage from Company Accounts.* London: Random House, 1996

11. "China beats America to the world's fastest supercomputer title - and it's faster than 338 MILLION ordinary PCs put together", *Daily Mail*, 17 June 2013

Index